Adolescent Sleep Needs and School Starting Times

EDITED BY
KYLA L. WAHLSTROM

Phi Delta Kappa Educational Foundation
Bloomington, Indiana U.S.A.

Cover illustration by Brenda Grannan
Cover design by Victoria Voelker

Phi Delta Kappa Educational Foundation
408 North Union Street
Post Office Box 789
Bloomington, Indiana 47402-0789
U.S.A.

Printed in the United States of America

Library of Congress Catalog Card Number 99-74230
ISBN 0-87367-817-6

TABLE OF CONTENTS

PREFACE

The primary focus of education is to maximize human potential. Therefore a key task for schools is to ensure that the conditions in which learning is to take place "address the very biology of our learners," as Mary Carskadon puts it in her article. At the heart of this matter is sleep, in particular adolescents' need for sleep versus societal demands, such as school starting times.

Few educators would argue that there are still many questions to be answered about the consequences — for good or ill — of altering school starting times in order to better address adolescents' need for sleep. But the battlelines are being drawn. Information can be both weapon and shield.

This book is a collection of five informative articles on adolescent sleep needs and school starting times that appeared in a special section of the *Phi Delta Kappan* in January 1999. The guest editor for that section was Kyla L. Wahlstrom, associate director of the Center for Applied Research and Educational Improvement at the University of Minnesota in Minneapolis. She kindly consented to serve as editor again for this collection.

Our hope is that this group of articles will prove to be a useful resource for teachers, administrators, parents, and others interested in this issue. At the back of this book, readers also will find information about ordering a 30-minute videotape in which Kyla Wahlstrom follows up on her article and amplifies many of the points discussed in print.

Donovan R. Walling
Editor of Special Publications

1

The Prickly Politics of School Starting Times

KYLA L. WAHLSTROM

Kyla L. Wahlstrom is associate director of the Center for Applied Research and Educational Improvement, University of Minnesota, Minneapolis.

Some school districts have responded to recent research findings on adolescent sleep patterns and needs by significantly changing high school starting times. Other districts are considering such a move. But tinkering with the school-day schedule is not without its risks.

Aware of those risks, in the fall of 1996 several superintendents of suburban Minnesota school districts asked the Center for Applied Research and Educational Improvement (CAREI) at the University of Minnesota to assess the attitudes of stakeholders toward such a venture. Seventeen school districts agreed to participate in the study, which soon focused not only on high schools but also on elementary and middle/junior high schools, since the schedules of all buildings in a district are inextricably linked.[1]

Of the 17 districts, only one of them — Edina — had already made the decision to start the high school day 70 minutes later in 1996-97 than in the previous school year. At the start of the study, then, only the stakeholders in Edina were actually experiencing the change. A year later, the Minneapolis School District pushed back the starting time of its seven comprehensive high schools by an hour and 25 minutes, from 7:15 to 8:40 a.m., enabling CAREI to study the actual impact of a later starting time in that district as well.[2]

The CAREI researchers discovered that changing a school's starting time provokes the same kind of emotional reaction from stakeholders as closing a school or changing a school's attendance area. A school's starting time sets the rhythm of the day for teachers, parents, students, and members of the community at large. The impact of changing that starting time is felt individually, and the individuals who are affected need to have their views heard and legitimized so that the discussion can move forward in search of common ground.

Another striking finding from the first year of the CAREI study had to do with the role that assumptions play in discussions of changing school starting times. Informal conversations on the topic seemed invariably to include a comment such as "The transportation department rules the district, and this change cannot take place because of bus problems" or "The coaches will never go along with this idea — there's no use in even approaching them."

To assess the accuracy of these and similar assumptions, we conducted individual interviews during the first year of the study with each participating district's transportation director, with 51 coaches and co-curricular faculty advisors, with all 17 district directors of community education, with several food service directors, with several district personnel directors, with all elementary and secondary curriculum directors, and with local employers who provide after-school jobs for students. Surprisingly, none of the interviewees suggested that a change in school starting time — especially at the high school level — would be out of the question. Indeed, though coaches and transportation directors did voice some concerns, most respondents in all categories were willing to discuss at length ways of implementing such a change, since it would be beneficial for students and their learning. To allow untested assumptions to forestall debate on the issue is to close the door prematurely (and possibly wrongly) to later starting times for high school students.

The CAREI study showed, too, that advocates for later school starting times tended to use in their lobbying efforts both hard data (e.g., the findings of sleep research on adolescents) and testimonials (e.g., positive outcomes from districts that had already made such a change). In both Edina and Minneapolis, a small number of advocates had a positive impact on the decision-making process.

It's important to remember, however, that strident advocacy can squelch debate. And without thorough discussion of the issues surrounding a proposed change in school starting time, any decision will be shallow and may have to be revisited.

In both Edina and Minneapolis, shifts in high school starting times affected the starting times of elementary and middle schools as well. Had the school board members in either of those districts focused solely on the logistics of the change, it is very unlikely that a later high school starting time would have been implemented. But the school boards in both districts first considered the research data on adolescent sleep needs. To their credit, they posed the question, Are the data of sufficient quality and relevance to merit consideration?

With that question answered affirmatively, the next questions became: What do we hope to gain by shifting our high school starting time? And what might we lose in the process? The answers to these two questions had to be based on fact, not on emotion or on potential logistical problems.

Eventually, however, both school boards arrived at the point where concerns about logistics appropriately entered the debate. Then the question became, What will it take to bring our school schedules into line with what the research tells us about adolescent sleep needs? The boards formed several subcommittees to investigate logistical problems and to come up with possible scenarios. Throughout the decision-making process, though, factual evidence took precedence, and students' best interests held sway. As a result, the discussions involved much less wrangling than has been seen in other districts embroiled in the same debate. From a school board's perspective, keeping a potentially divisive debate focused on student needs is good politics.

If altering high school starting times is risky for school boards, it is equally risky for superintendents. In an open forum, the 17 superintendents whose districts took part in the CAREI study discussed the dissension that community debate on the topic had caused in some locales. Three superintendents, in whose districts the topic had not surfaced, said they did not plan to bring it up. Two of the three noted that their contracts were up for renewal, and they did not want their boards split over this potentially divisive issue (on which they would be forced to take a stand). They elected instead to remain publicly silent and privately neutral on the topic.

In Minneapolis, the decision to move to a later starting time for the high schools was made under an interim superintendent. When the new superintendent took over, she "inherited" that decision, and any perceived negatives related to its implementation were not associated with her.

If altering school starting times is risky for school boards and superintendents, it is no less so for high school principals. In Edina and Minneapolis, the high school principals served on the committees that made the decision to push back high school starting times. Like other committee members, these principals had access to the sleep research data and to information on outcomes from districts that had already taken such action. Armed with the facts, the principals were able to refute unsubstantiated claims and to respond to the concerns of students, parents, and teachers. Participation in the committees' debates also helped the high school principals identify potential sources of resistance to the change and learn to deal with them before opposition escalated.

It was equally important to have the elementary and middle/junior high school principals involved in the discussions, since changing the high school starting time inevitably affects other buildings as well. In large districts, however, it is impractical to have as many principals take part in the deliberations as might be optimal. Minneapolis compensated by providing regular briefings on the committees' discussions to all principals in the district.

Clearly, schools at all levels whose own schedules will be affected by a change in the high school starting time must be given sufficient advance notice. In Minneapolis, schools that were told in the spring that their starting times would be changed in the fall encountered much less resistance from parents and staff members than did schools that learned about the change shortly before the fall term began. Staff members and parents need time to adjust their personal and family schedules, and providing such time is one key to a smooth transition.

All the findings of the CAREI study that I have mentioned so far apply to both urban and suburban schools and school districts. But a few factors emerged that seem more pertinent to one setting than to the other.

The reactions of high school teachers to a later starting time differed by setting, for example. A clear majority of the suburban teachers said that they liked the change, for reasons that ranged from "more time to incorporate the news of the day into my lessons" and "more students are awake and fully participating in my first- and second-hour classes" to "more time to talk with fellow teachers about sharing materials and team teaching." The suburban teachers were still arriving at an early hour — but, because of the later dismissal time, they were working a longer day.

Urban high school teachers, by contrast, were evenly split between liking (45.2%) and not liking (45.7%) the later starting time. Those who responded positively to the change cited many of the same reasons listed by their suburban counterparts. But two-thirds of the urban teachers who did not like the change mentioned the negative impact that a later dismissal time had on their personal lives. Their comments ranged from "I feel I have no 'down time' before I go home" and "I have lost at least an hour that I would otherwise spend at my second job" to "I now have to face rush-hour traffic." Only one-third of the teachers who disliked the change mentioned the needs of students in their listings of negative concerns.

These sharp differences in teachers' attitudes deserve further study. Perhaps urban teachers are simply reflecting the stresses of teaching under less than ideal conditions. The personal toll of having to make accommodations for a later starting time may be the final straw that makes this change feel overwhelming.

The preferred dismissal time for elementary and middle/junior high schools is another factor that differs by locale. Parents in both suburban and urban areas worry about young children walking along roads or waiting for a bus at a road's edge in winter darkness. But urban parents worry too that "there's a different kind of predator out there in the late afternoon." Thus urban parents prefer an earlier school dismissal time to a later one.

A third issue that differs by locale is "zero hour" classes — those that meet an hour before the regular school day begins. Such classes are usually limited in enrollment, since they serve accelerated students or youngsters in work/study programs. The CAREI study reveals that more suburban students than urban ones take zero hour classes, because transportation to school is less of a problem in suburban areas. This equity issue merits further study.

Moreover, zero hour classes negate for participants the beneficial effects of a later school starting time. Districts may wish to consider the wisdom of offering such options.

Obviously, changing a high school's starting time produces a complex array of benefits and tensions. Just as clearly, districts must challenge the assumptions before a genuine dialogue can take place on the topic.

Meanwhile, we still do not know the effect of a later high school starting time on student achievement. In an effort to provide that information, CAREI is now looking at longitudinal achievement data from districts that implemented a later starting time several years ago.

CAREI will also seek to answer the question of whether a later high school starting time reduces the incidence of juvenile misbehavior by keeping youngsters in school until later in the afternoon. To date, there is no evidence to suggest that crime rates have dropped as a result of pushing back school starting times.

CAREI has studied most extensively the two Minnesota districts that have pushed back their high school starting times by an hour or more. Other districts in the state have implemented a 30- to 40-minute delay in the start of school. Still other districts have accepted the value of a later starting time but are struggling in committees over how to deal with the logistical problems. Meanwhile, CAREI researchers are looking for an answer to the question, How late is late enough to help address the sleep needs of adolescents without changing school schedules more than is necessary?

High school starting time is a seemingly simple issue with prickly political dimensions, and there is no single solution that will fit all districts. Only through open discussion of their concerns can stakeholders develop a shared understanding of the facts that will lead to a reasonable — but purely local — decision. And that's as it should be, since those stakeholders are the ones who will have to live with the consequences.

Notes

1. Kyla Wahlstrom and Carol Freeman, "Executive Summary of Findings from School Start Time Study," 1997, available from http://carei. coled.umn.edu.
2. Kyla Wahlstrom, Gordon Wrobel, and Patricia Kubow, "Executive Summary of Findings from Minneapolis School District School Start Time Study," 1998, available from http://carei.coled.umn.edu.

When Worlds Collide: Adolescent Need for Sleep Versus Societal Demands

MARY A. CARSKADON

Mary A. Carskadon is a professor of psychiatry and human behavior at the Brown University School of Medicine and director of sleep and chronobiology research at E.P. Bradley Hospital, East Providence, Rhode Island. The research summarized in this article was supported by grants from the National Institutes of Health (MH52415, NR04270, MH01358, and MH45945) and aided by the efforts of many colleagues and collaborators.

Our understanding of the development of sleep patterns in adolescents has advanced considerably in the last 20 years. Along the way, theoretical models of the processes underlying the biological regulation of sleep have improved, and certain assumptions and dogmas have been examined and found wanting. Although the full characterization of teen sleep regulation remains to be accomplished, our current understanding poses a number of challenges for the education system.

The early 1970s found us with a growing awareness that sleep patterns change fundamentally at the transition to adolescence — a phenomenon that is widely acknowledged today. Survey studies clearly showed then and continue to show that the reported timing of sleep begins to shift in early adolescence, with bedtime and rising time both occurring at later hours. This delayed sleep pattern is particularly evident on nonschool nights and days, though the evening delay is obvious on school nights as well. Associated with the delay of sleep is a decline in the amount of sleep obtained and an increase in the discrepancy between school nights and weekend nights. Although the nonschool-night "over-sleeping" was acknowledged as recovery from insufficient sleep during the school week, we initially assumed that the amount of sleep required declines with age. This was axiomatic: the older you are, the less sleep you need.

Assessing the Need for Sleep in the Second Decade

A longitudinal study begun in 1976 at the Stanford University summer sleep camp attempted to examine this axiom.[1] Boys and girls enrolled in this research project at ages 10, 11, or 12 and came to the lab for a 72-hour assessment each year for five or six years. They were asked to keep a fixed schedule, sleeping 10 hours a night for the week before the study, and their sleep was recorded on three consecutive nights from 10 p.m. to 8 a.m. Our hypothesis was that the reduced need for sleep in older children would manifest itself through less sleep within this 10-hour nocturnal window. This hypothesis was *not* confirmed. In fact, regardless of age or developmental stage, the children all slept about 9¼ of the 10 hours. Furthermore, delays in sleep resulted in a reduced likelihood of spontaneous waking before 8 a.m. for all but the youngest participants. One conclusion, therefore, was that the need for sleep does not change across adolescent development.

This study also showed an interesting pattern with respect to waking alertness, which was assessed using a technique called the Multiple Sleep Latency Test (MSLT). The MSLT measures the speed of falling asleep across repeated 20-minute trials in standard conditions. Thus a child who stays awake 20 minutes can be considered alert, faster sleep onsets are a sign of reduced alertness, and a child who falls asleep in five minutes or less is

excessively sleepy.[2] The longitudinal study demonstrated that —
even though the total amount of sleep was unchanged — alertness declined in association with pubertal development.[3] Figure 1
illustrates the MSLT patterns: under these experimental conditions, more mature adolescents showed signs of reduced alertness
even though they slept an equivalent amount at night. One interpretation of these data is that older teenagers may need *more*
sleep than when they were younger. On the other hand, the pattern of sleep tendency showing a midafternoon dip may reflect
maturation of a regulated behavioral pattern favoring an afternoon nap or siesta.

FIGURE 1.

**Developmental Change in Daytime Alertness Under
Conditions of 'Optimal' Sleep**

The upper line, labeled Tanner 1-2, shows that pre- and early-pubescent
boys and girls with a 10-hour sleep opportunity are not at all sleepy. The
lower line, labeled Tanner 3-5, shows that more physically mature
youngsters are sleepier, even though they have the same sleep opportunity.

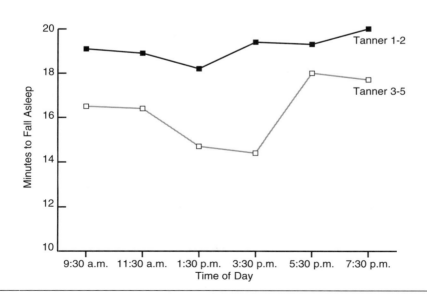

Behavioral Factors

The principle that adolescents sleep later and less because of a panoply of psychosocial factors was also axiomatic during the 1970s and the 1980s. The evidence for this included a change in parental involvement in youngsters' sleep schedules as the children age. Thus, until about ages 11 or 12, more children than not reported that they woke spontaneously in the morning and that parents set their bedtimes. Fewer children in their early teens reported that parents still set their bedtimes, and most said that they required an alarm clock or a parent to assist them in waking up.[4]

Other behavioral factors contributing to the changing sleep patterns with age include increased social opportunities and growing academic demands. Another major contributor to changing adolescent sleep patterns is employment. One survey of youngsters in New England in the late 1980s found that two-thirds of high school students had jobs and that nearly 30% worked 20 or more hours in a typical school week.[5] Those high school students who worked 20 hours or more reported later bedtimes, shorter sleep times, more frequent episodes of falling asleep in school, and more frequent oversleeping and arriving late at school.

In addition to changing parental involvement, increasing school and social obligations, and greater participation in the work force, there are a myriad of other phenomena that have not been well explored. Access in the bedroom to computers, televisions, telephones, and so forth probably contributes to the delay of and reduction in sleep.

Another factor that has a major influence on adolescent sleep is the school schedule. The starting time of school puts limits on the time available for sleep. This is a nonnegotiable limit established largely without concern for sleep. Most school districts set the earliest starting time for older adolescents and the latest starting time for younger children. District officials commonly acknowledge that the school schedule is determined by the availability of school buses, along with such other factors as time of

14

local sunrise, sports teams' schedules, and so forth. As described in other articles in this special section, concerns about the impact of school schedules on sleep patterns (as well as concerns about after-school teen delinquency) have sparked a reexamination in a number of districts. Our studies indicate that such a reexamination is merited by the difficulties many teenagers experience.

Biological Factors

As findings of the tendency for adolescent sleep patterns to be delayed were reported not only in North America but also in South America, Asia, Australia, and Europe, a sense arose that intrinsic developmental changes may also play a role in this phenomenon.[6] At the same time, conceptual models of the underlying internal mechanisms that control the length and timing of sleep began to take shape.

Current models posit three factors that control human sleep patterns. One of these factors is behavior and includes external factors such as those discussed above. The intrinsic factors have been called "sleep/wake homeostasis" and the "circadian timing system," or "process S" and "process C" in one model.[7] Sleep/wake homeostasis more simply stated is that sleep favors wake and wake favors sleep. All other things being equal, therefore, the longer one is awake, the greater the pressure for sleep to occur. Conversely, the closer one is to having slept, the less pressure there is to sleep. This process accounts for the increased need for sleep after staying awake all night and the difficulty of staying awake in general when faced with a chronic pattern of insufficient sleep. Process S can be examined using measures of sleep tendency, such as the MSLT, or measures of EEG (electroencephalogram) slow wave activity (SWA) during sleep. Sleep tendency and SWA increase with insufficient sleep. Both factors also show changes across adolescent development that may be related to the timing of sleep.

Under conditions of optimal sleep, such as those described in the longitudinal study of sleep, slow wave sleep declines by 40%

from early to late adolescence. This decline may indicate a reduced pressure for sleep with greater maturation. One interpretation of this finding is that the reduced pressure for sleep makes staying up late an easier task for older adolescents. Others have interpreted this finding as marking a structural change in the brain (thinning of cortical synaptic density) that is unrelated to sleep/wake homeostasis. The change in sleep tendency — that is, the appearance of a midday trough at midpuberty (Figure 1) — may indicate a reorganization of the sleep/wake homeostatic mechanism to favor daytime napping and an extended late-day waking period, again favoring a later bedtime. These hypotheses are speculative and require additional study.

Much of the contemporary excitement about adolescent sleep comes from studies of the circadian timing mechanism, which independently and interactively exerts influences on sleep through processes that favor or inhibit sleep according to the dictates of an internal biological "clock." Several features of the human circadian timing system and its interactions with sleep and wakefulness are relevant here.

- Circadian rhythms are biological oscillations with periods of about 24 hours.
- Circadian rhythms are synchronized to the 24-hour day chiefly by light signals.
- The chief circadian oscillator in mammals is located deep within the brain in the suprachiasmatic nuclei (SCN) of the hypothalamus.
- Circadian rhythms can be assessed by measuring the timing of biological events.
- Circadian rhythms are thought to control the timing of "sleep gates" and "forbidden zones" for sleep.
- Circadian rhythms control the timing of REM (rapid eye movement) sleep within the sleep period.

A first attempt to examine whether the circadian timing system undergoes developmental changes during adolescent maturation involved a survey of sixth-grade girls. In this survey, one series of questions allowed us to estimate physical development and another series gave a measure of circadian phase preference. Phase preference refers to an individual's tendency to favor activities in the morning or evening, i.e., morningness/eveningness. In these 275 sixth-grade girls, the puberty score and circadian phase preference score showed a significant relationship: less mature girls favored earlier hours, and more mature girls favored later hours.[8] These data were the first to implicate a biological process in the later timing of adolescent sleep; however, the measures were indirect and self-reported.

Our subsequent studies have attempted to confirm a pubertally mediated phase delay in adolescents using more precise measures. For example, one of the best ways to identify time in the intrinsic biological clock in humans is to examine melatonin secretion.[9] Melatonin is a hormone that is produced by the pineal gland and regulated by the circadian timing system. Melatonin secretion occurs during nocturnal hours in both day-active species, like humans, and night-active species. Melatonin can be measured from saliva samples collected in dim lighting conditions. The normal melatonin curve in dim light provides a very robust signal, as shown in Figure 2 on the next page.

Because the intrinsic circadian timing system is synchronized to the 24-hour cycle principally by light (even in humans), careful evaluation of the relationship between the endogenous cycle and the developmental phase must control for or eliminate behavioral differences, such as later bedtimes, that affect the timing of light the internal clock receives. Hence, we developed an experimental protocol to incorporate such controls by placing adolescents on identical light/dark schedules. Under strictly controlled conditions, we found a significant correlation between pubertal development (which can be evaluated by trained physicians or nurses using markers of secondary sexual characteristics[10]) and circadian timing: more mature adolescents had a later timing of the termination of melatonin secretion.[11]

Current and planned investigations need to examine mechanisms for this pattern and to determine more clearly how the cir-

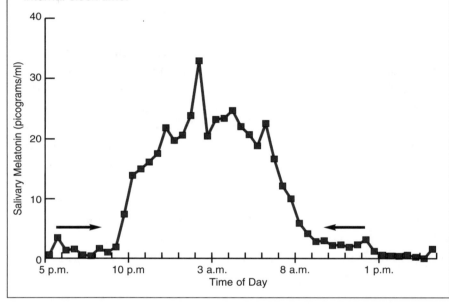

FIGURE 2.
Pattern of Melatonin Secretion (Measured in Saliva Samples)

Melatonin secretion has a sharp onset and relatively sharp offset. The arrows indicate times at which onset and offset of melatonin secretion occur in adolescents who keep a very strict schedule, going to bed at 10 p.m and waking at 8 a.m. The secretion of melatonin is controlled by the circadian timing system and is an excellent measure for determining internal clock time.

cadian timing system is linked to the sleep/wake system during development. One approach to this inquiry uses an elegant experimental design in which youngsters are placed on a sleep/wake schedule that is outside the range of values capable of synchronizing the internal clock. In this experiment, bedtime and rising time are scheduled four hours later from one day to the next, effecting a 28-hour day. Because the internal clock cannot accommodate to this demand, it runs free at its own intrinsic day length. This measure itself can provide crucial evidence about adolescent timing in the 24-hour world. According to circadian rhythms theory, adolescents with long internal day lengths will synchronize to the external day with a later alignment than adolescents with shorter internal day lengths.

In such a study, we can also evaluate sleeping and waking measures occurring at every phase of the circadian cycle and at every time since the participant fell asleep or woke up. In other words, we are able to examine the independent influences of the circadian timing system and the sleep/wake homeostatic process and their interactions. When we evaluated the sleep tendency of adolescents using the MSLT measured in the 28-hour day, we found that the circadian pressure to sleep — regardless of how long an individual had been awake — was greatest right as the melatonin secretion was about to turn off, about an hour before "normal" waking up time; the circadian pressure to stay awake was greatest right before melatonin secretion was about to begin, about an hour before "normal" bedtime.[12] Taken alone, this is a curious finding, because one ordinarily experiences sleep pressure to be greatest at bedtime and least on waking up.

On the other hand, when we examined sleep tendency as a function of how long the participants had been awake — regardless of circadian time — the lowest sleep pressure occurred close to rising time and the greatest sleep pressure at the end of the waking period. When examined in combination, these two processes provide an explanation for humans' ability to experience an extended wakeful period. When viewed as opposing processes,[13] sleep/wake homeostasis provides for alertness early in the day, when the circadian timing mechanism favors sleep, and the circadian timing system props up alertness late in the day, when the homeostatic process favors sleep. In the context of adolescent development, if there is a situation in which sleep pressure builds more slowly or circadian timing is delayed or both, adolescents will encounter a "forbidden zone" for sleep later in the day.

Other facets of the circadian timing system that may influence the later timing of sleep behavior in adolescents include a potentially greater sensitivity to low light levels in the evening. Such a sensitivity could affect the circadian timing system by pushing the forbidden zone for sleep to a later time. The mechanism for such an effect is described in the phase response curve, in which light to the internal clock late in the evening pushes the clock to a later time and light to the internal clock early in the morning pushes the clock to an earlier time. The characteristics of this circadian phase resetting mechanism may also change during adolescent maturation.

One other important finding from our studies is that the circadian timing system can be reset if light exposure is carefully controlled. In many of our studies, we require adolescents to keep a specific sleep schedule (for example, 10 p.m. to 8 a.m.) and to wear eyeshades to exclude light during these hours. In fact, we pay adolescents to keep this schedule! When we measure melatonin secretion before the students go on the new schedule (when they are still on their self-selected routine) and again after 10 or 11 nights on the new schedule, we find that the melatonin secretion has moved significantly toward a common time: those who were early melatonin secretors move to a later time, and those who were late secretors move earlier.[14] Thus we know that the system is not immutable; with time, effort, *and* money, we can get adolescents to realign their rhythms!

Let us summarize what we now know about the developmental trends in adolescent sleep behavior and adolescents' sleep/wake and circadian systems.

- As they mature, adolescents tend to go to bed later and to wake up later (given the opportunity).
- Adolescents also tend to sleep less as they mature.
- The difference between the amount and timing of sleep on weekend nights versus school nights grows during adolescence.
- These trends are apparent in adolescents both in North America and in industrialized countries on other continents.
- Sleep requirements do not decline during adolescent development.
- Daytime sleep tendency is augmented during puberty.

- The timing of events controlled by the circadian timing system is delayed during puberty.

We propose that the delay of sleep during adolescent development is favored by behavioral and intrinsic processes and that the reduction of sleep experienced by adolescents is largely driven by a collision between the intrinsic processes and the expectations and demands of the adult world. The study described in the following section illustrates this point.

School Transition Project

Our school transition project took a look at what happened to sleep and circadian rhythms in a group of youngsters for whom the transition from junior high school to senior high school required a change in the starting time for school from 8:25 a.m. to 7:20 a.m. Twenty-five youngsters completed our study at two time points, in the spring of the ninth grade and in the autumn of the 10th grade.[15] These boys and girls were all well beyond the beginning changes of puberty; some were physically mature. They were enrolled in the study with instructions simply to keep their usual schedules, to wear small activity monitors on their wrists, and to keep diaries of their activities and sleep schedule for two consecutive weeks. At the end of the two weeks, participants came to the sleep laboratory for assessment of the onset phase of melatonin secretion, overnight sleep study, and daytime testing with the MSLT. The laboratory sleep schedule was fixed to each student's average school-night schedule based on the data from the wrist monitor (actigraph).

As predicted, the actigraph data showed that students woke up earlier when confronted with the 7:20 a.m. start time, although rising time was on average only about 25 minutes earlier (6:26 a.m. to 6:01 a.m.), not the 65 minutes represented by the school schedule change. Sleep onset times did not change, averaging about 10:40 p.m. in both grades. The average amount of sleep on school nights fell from seven hours and nine minutes to six hours and 50 minutes, a statistically significant amount and probably a meaningful amount when considered as producing an ever cumulating sleep deficit.

The amount of sleep these students obtained in ninth grade was below the amount we feel is required for optimal alertness, and the further decline in 10th grade had added impact. One way to examine the impact is to look at the MSLT data from tests that occurred at 9:30 a.m., 10:30 a.m., 12:30 p.m., and 2:30 p.m. If we look at comparable MSLT data from Figure 1, we find an average score of 18.9 minutes for the early pubertal children and 15.5 minutes for the mid- to late pubertal adolescents sleeping on the optimizing 10-hour schedule. The ninth-grade students in this more naturalistic study, by contrast, had an average MSLT speed of falling asleep of 11.4 minutes, and in 10th grade the sleep score was 8.5 minutes. In clinical terms, these students were in a borderline zone for daytime sleepiness, well below the alert range and below the "normal" range, yet not in the "pathological" range.

A closer look at the MSLT test results shows that the students in 10th grade were in the pathological range when tested at 8:30 a.m. (MSLT score = 5.1 minutes). Furthermore, nearly 50% of these 10th-graders showed a reversed sleep pattern on the morning MSLT tests that is similar to the pattern seen in patients with the sleep disorder called narcolepsy — that is, REM sleep occurs before non-REM sleep. The 12 students who showed this "narcoleptic" pattern fell asleep in an average of 3.4 minutes when tested at 8:30 a.m. These students did not have narcolepsy; what they did have was a significant mismatch between their circadian rhythms and the necessity to get up and go to school. The evidence for this mismatch was a later time for the onset of melatonin secretion compared with those who did not have the "narcoleptic" pattern: 9:46 p.m. versus 8:36 p.m. This marker of the circadian timing system indicates that 1) the students' natural time to fall asleep is about 11 p.m. or later (on average) and 2) the abnormally short time to sleep onset on the 8:30 a.m. MSLT and the abnormal occurrence of REM sleep took place because the students were tested at the very nadir of their circadian day. In other words, at 8:30 a.m., these students' brains were far better suited to be asleep than awake!

Why were these 12 students so different from the others? We were unable to identify a specific cause. None of the 25 students made an optimal adjustment to the new schedule; none was sleeping even as much as 8¼ hours on school nights, a value we suggest elsewhere might be adequate if not optimal for high school students.[16] A few students maintained a "normal" level of alertness, others were borderline, and still others were in the pathological range. The 12 students whose circadian timing systems moved to a much later timing in 10th grade, however, showed signs associated with marked impairment, particularly in the morning hours.

Consequences, Concerns, and Countermeasures

Among the known consequences of insufficient sleep are memory lapses, attentional deficits, depressed mood, and slowed reaction time. Sleep deprivation studies have shown that divergent thinking suffers with inadequate sleep. A few surveys have noted poorer grades in students with inadequate sleep. Many important issues have not yet been well studied. For example, little is known about the consequences of insufficient sleep for relationship formation and maintenance, emotion regulation, delinquency, drug use, and violent behavior. Long-term consequences of insufficient sleep — particularly at critical developmental stages — are utterly unknown.

The problem of inadequate sleep affects more segments of our society than adolescents; however, adolescents appear to be particularly vulnerable and face difficult challenges for obtaining sufficient sleep. Even without the pressure of biological changes, if we combine an early school starting time — say 7:30 a.m., which, with a modest commute, makes 6:15 a.m. a viable rising time — with our knowledge that optimal sleep need is 9¼ hours, we are asking that 16-year-olds go to bed at 9 p.m. Rare is the teenager of the 1990s who will keep such a schedule. School work, sports practices, clubs, volunteer work, and paid employment take precedence. When biological changes are factored in, the ability even to have merely "adequate" sleep is lost. As a consequence, sleepy teens demand that parents provide an extreme form of reveille, challenge teachers to offer maximal classroom entertainment and creativity just to keep them awake, and suffer the consequences of disaffection from school and dissatisfaction with themselves.

Can these problems be solved by delaying the starting time for school as adolescents move into the pubertal years? Not entirely. Moving the opening bell to a later time may help many teens with the mismatch between biological time and scholastic time, but it will not provide more hours in the day. It is not difficult to project that a large number of students see a later starting time as permission to stay up later at night studying, working, surfing the net, watching television, and so forth. Today's teens know little about their sleep needs or about the biological timing system. Interestingly, students do know they are sleepy, but they do not have skills to cope with the issue, and many assume — just as adults do — that they are expected to function with an inadequate amount of sleep. This assumption is a physiological fallacy: sleep is not optional. Sleep is biologically obligatory. If students learn about sleep, they have a basis to use a changed school starting time to best advantage. Adding information about sleep to the school curriculum can certainly help.

As with other fields of scientific investigation, the knowledge base, the scientific opportunities, and the level of pure excitement in sleep and biological rhythms research have never been greater. This knowledge and excitement can be shared with students at every academic level. Furthermore, sleep and biological rhythms are natural gateways to learning because students are drawn to the topics. Thus, as grammar school students learn about the nutrition pyramid, so too could they learn about the body's sleep requirements and how the biological timing system makes humans day-active rather than night-active. (Did you know that, if you put your hamster in a box with lights that turn on at night and off in the day-time, it will start running on its wheel during the day?)

As middle school students are learning about comparative biology, they can be sharing in the excitement of where, when, and how animals sleep. (Did you know that certain dolphins can be half asleep . . . literally? One half of the brain sleeps while the other half is awake! Did you know that mammals stop regulating body temperature in REM sleep? Did you know that you are paralyzed in REM sleep?)

High school students can share the excitement in the discoveries about genes that control the biological clock, about the brain mechanisms that control dreaming, about the way sleep creates breathing problems, and about sleep disorders that may affect their family members. (Did you know that snoring may be a sign of a serious sleep disorder afflicting as many as 5% of adults? Did you know that some people act out their dreams at night? Did you know that genes controlling the biological clock in mice and fruit flies are nearly identical?)

Challenges and an Opportunity

The challenges are great, and solutions do not come easily. School scheduling is incredibly complex, and accounting for youngsters' sleep needs and biological propensities adds to the complexity. Yet we cannot assume that the system is immutable. Given that the primary focus of education is to maximize human potential, then a new task before us is to ensure that the conditions in which learning takes place address the very biology of our learners.

Notes

1. Mary A. Carskadon, "Determinants of Daytime Sleepiness: Adolescent Development, Extended and Restricted Nocturnal Sleep" (Doctoral dissertation, Stanford University, 1979); idem, "The Second Decade," in Christian Guilleminault, ed., *Sleeping and Waking Disorders: Indications and Techniques* (Menlo Park, Calif.: Addison Wesley, 1982), pp. 99-125; and Mary A. Carskadon, E. John Orav, and William C. Dement, "Evolution of Sleep and Daytime Sleepiness in Adolescents," in Christian Guilleminault and Elio Lugaresi, eds., *Sleep/Wake Disorders: Natural History,*

Epidemiology, and Long-Term Evolution (New York: Raven Press, 1983), pp. 201-16.

2. Mary A. Carskadon and William C. Dement, "The Multiple Sleep Latency Test: What Does It Measure?" *Sleep*, vol. 5, 1982, pp. 67-72.

3. Mary A. Carskadon et al., "Pubertal Changes in Daytime Sleepiness," *Sleep*, vol. 2, 1980, pp. 453-60.

4. Carskadon, "Determinants of Daytime Sleepiness."

5. Mary A. Carskadon, "Patterns of Sleep and Sleepiness in Adolescents," *Pediatrician*, vol. 17, 1990, pp. 5-12.

6. Mirian M. M. Andrade and Luiz Menna-Barreto, "Sleep Patterns of High School Students Living in São Paulo, Brazil," in Mary A. Carskadon, ed., *Adolescent Sleep Patterns: Biological, Social, and Psychological Influences* (New York: Cambridge University Press, forthcoming); Kaneyoshi Ishihara, Yukako Honma, and Susumu Miyake, "Investigation of the Children's Version of the Morningness-Eveningness Questionnaire with Primary and Junior High School Pupils in Japan," *Perceptual and Motor Skills*, vol. 71, 1990, pp. 1353-54; Helen M. Bearpark and Patricia T. Michie, "Prevalence of Sleep/Wake Disturbances in Sidney Adolescents," *Sleep Research*, vol. 16, 1987, p. 304; and Inge Strauch and Barbara Meier, "Sleep Need in Adolescents: A Longitudinal Approach," *Sleep*, vol. 11, 1988, pp. 378-86.

7. Alexander A. Borbély, "A Two Process Model of Sleep Regulation," *Human Neurobiology*, vol. 1, 1982, pp. 195-204.

8. Mary A. Carskadon, Cecilia Vieira, and Christine Acebo, "Association Between Puberty and Delayed Phase Preference," *Sleep*, vol. 16, 1993, pp. 258-62.

9. Alfred J. Lewy and Robert L. Sack, "The Dim Light Melatonin Onset as a Marker for Circadian Phase Position," *Chronobiology International*, vol. 6, 1989, pp. 93-102.

10. J. M. Tanner, *Growth at Adolescence*, 2nd ed. (Oxford: Blackwell, 1962).

11. Mary A. Carskadon et al., "An Approach to Studying Circadian Rhythms of Adolescent Humans," *Journal of Biological Rhythms*, vol. 12, 1997, pp. 278-89.

12. Mary A. Carskadon et al., "Circadian and Homeostatic Influences on Sleep Latency in Adolescents," paper presented at the sixth

meeting of the Society for Research on Biological Rhythms, Amelia Island Plantations, 1998.

13. Dale M. Edgar, William C. Dement, and Charles A. Fuller, "Effect of SCN Lesions on Sleep in Squirrel Monkeys — Evidence for Opponent Processes in Sleep-Wake Regulation," *Journal of Neuroscience*, vol. 13, 1993, pp. 1065-79.

14. Carskadon et al., "An Approach to Studying Circadian Rhythms."

15. Mary A. Carskadon et al., "Adolescent Sleep Patterns, Circadian Timing, and Sleepiness at a Transition to Early School Days," *Sleep*, in press.

16. Amy R. Wolfson and Mary A. Carskadon, "Sleep Schedules and Daytime Functioning in Adolescents," *Child Development*, vol. 69, 1998, pp. 875-87.

The Consequences of Insufficient Sleep for Adolescents: Links Between Sleep and Emotional Regulation

RONALD E. DAHL, M.D.

Ronald E. Dahl, M.D., is an associate professor of psychiatry and pediatrics at the University of Pittsburgh Medical Center, Pittsburgh, Pennsylvania.

A dolescents often "get by" with relatively little sleep, but it may be far less than they need. The observations of many parents, educators, and clinicians are in close agreement with a wealth of scientific data about the growing frequency of this worrisome pattern of behavior. As discussed in other articles in this special section, there has been recent progress in understanding many of the factors that contribute to adolescent sleep loss, including the role of early school starting times and the role of various biological and social influences on adolescents' self-selected bedtimes.

The increasing evidence that teenagers seem to be getting less sleep leads inevitably to the pragmatic question "How much sleep do adolescents really need?" Unfortunately, the medical/scientific answer to this question seems tautological. Sufficient sleep is defined as "the amount necessary to permit optimal day-time functioning."

As impractical as that answer may appear, there are two important reasons for such a definition. First, sleep requirements can be remarkably different across individuals. Second, at a physiological level, sleep and waking states are closely intertwined aspects of a larger system of arousal regulation. (Sleep researchers often use the Chinese symbol of yin/yang to designate the interrelationship of sleep/wake states.)

At the center of this discussion is a critical and pragmatic point: any evaluation of the sleep habits of adolescents must include a careful consideration of the *waking consequences* of sleep loss. The question becomes, in essence, "What are the daytime signs of diminished functioning that indicate insufficient sleep?" While there is a shortage of well-controlled research studies that seek to answer this question, this article focuses on the convergence of evidence suggesting that *changes in mood and motivation are among the most important effects of sleep loss*. Thus an important place to begin looking for evidence of insufficient sleep among adolescents is in the area of emotional or behavioral difficulties.

There is no shortage of epidemiological and clinical studies documenting recent increases in the rates of many psychiatric disorders among adolescents. Certainly many complex factors are likely to have contributed to the emotional and behavioral problems of teenagers, but the possible link to adolescent sleep patterns bears some scrutiny. There is clear evidence that sleep loss *can* lead to the development or exacerbation of behavioral and emotional problems.[1] The key question is "How great is the contribution of sleep deprivation to these problems?" The magnitude of this link remains an open question that can be answered only through careful empirical research.

In the meantime, these issues have enormous ramifications for the fields of medicine and education with regard both to the physical and mental health of adolescents and to detriments to effective learning and social development. Many policy decisions will be influenced by our understanding and interpretation of the importance of sleep in these areas.

In this article I provide an overview of current scientific and clinical information regarding the consequences of insufficient sleep in adolescents. I pay particular attention to links between sleep and emotional regulation. The following is a brief outline of the main points to be presented:

1. *Sleepiness*. This is the most direct consequence of adolescent sleep loss, and it manifests itself most significantly in difficulty getting up on time for school and in falling asleep in school. These problems can further contribute to conflicts with parents and teachers and to poor self-esteem. Sleepiness is also associated with a strong tendency toward brief mental lapses (or microsleeps) that greatly increase the risk of motor vehicle and other kinds of accidents.

2. *Tiredness*. This is a symptom of sleep loss and includes changes in motivation — particularly difficulty initiating behaviors related to long-term or abstract goals and decreased persistence in working toward goals.

3. *Mood, attention, and behavior*. Sleep loss can have negative effects on the control of mood, attention, and behavior. Irritability, moodiness, and low tolerance for frustration are the most frequently described symptoms in sleep-deprived adolescents. However, in some situations, sleepy teenagers are more likely to appear silly, impulsive, or sad.

4. *Impact of emotional and behavioral problems*. Emotional arousal and distress can cause both difficulty falling asleep and sleep disruptions. Behavioral problems and family chaos can contribute to even later bedtimes and to sleep schedules that are ever more incompatible with school schedules.

5. *Bi-directional effects*. There are bi-directional effects between sleep and behavioral/emotional problems. It can be difficult at times to identify the causal links. For example, a depressed adolescent with severe sleep problems may be showing sleep disturbances that stem from depression or mood problems that stem from sleep disruption. Sleep loss can also contribute to a negative

31

spiral or vicious cycle of deterioration. That is, sleep loss can have a negative effect on mood and behavior, which leads to subsequent emotional/behavioral difficulties that further interfere with sleep. This produces a sequence of negative effects in both domains. In some clinical cases, such negative spirals appear to be a pathway to withdrawal from school or serious psychiatric problems.

The Need for Sleep: An Overview

Before discussing the specific consequences of insufficient sleep in adolescents, it is necessary to begin with a general overview on what sleep is and why it is necessary at all.

Sleep is *not* simply rest. Mere rest does not create the restorative state of having slept. (Anyone who doubts this should try the following experiment tonight: spend eight hours resting in bed, with eyes closed, body relaxed, mind floating, in a deeply tranquil state, but without ever going to sleep; then keep track of your mood and performance tomorrow.) The fundamental difference between sleep and a deeply relaxed wakefulness is that sleep involves dropping into a state with a relative *loss of awareness of and responsiveness to the external world*. This state of unresponsiveness appears to be necessary for the restorative processes that occur during sleep to take place.

Furthermore, sleep itself is an *active* process. Sleep involves dynamically changing patterns and progressive stages, with some brain regions showing a great deal of activity in some sleep stages. Moreover, there are several aspects of sleep necessary for full restoration, including the continuity, timing, and patterning of different stages of sleep, as well as the timing of the sleep in relation to other biological rhythms.

For example, if subjects are permitted a full night's sleep but are awakened every 15 minutes for brief periods, on the following day they will report tiredness, fatigue, and emotional changes similar to having obtained insufficient amounts of sleep. Similarly, if subjects are permitted as much sleep as they need but are selectively deprived of one sleep stage — such as REM (rapid eye movement) sleep or delta sleep — they also report daytime consequences. And, as anyone who has experienced jet lag can attest, sleep that occurs at the wrong circadian phase is often fragmented and inefficient at restoration.

Sleep is not some biological luxury. Sleep is essential for basic survival, occurring in every species of living creature that has ever been studied. Animals deprived of sleep die. (Experiments with rats show that they can survive without sleep for about as long as they can survive without food.) Yet the specific function of sleep — *why* it is necessary for survival — remains a scientific mystery and the focus of a great deal of investigation.

Within this scientific mystery, however, are two important clues that are relevant to discussions of sleep and adolescent health. First, sleep seems to be particularly important during periods of brain maturation. (Across species, maturing individuals sleep more than fully mature individuals.) Second, sleep is naturally restricted to times and places that feel safe. Most species have evolved mechanisms to ensure that sleep is limited to such safe places as burrows and nests and to times of relative safety from predators. In humans, there is a similar tendency for safe feelings to promote sleep while feelings of threat or stress tend to inhibit sleep.

These links between sleep and stress are an important source of sleep disruption among adolescents. A key point can be best illustrated by a brief consideration of the evolutionary underpinnings of these biological links between sleep and emotion. For most of early human history, large nocturnal-hunting carnivores surrounded our ancestors, who had no access to physically safe sleep sites. (Humans cannot sleep in trees or on cliff edges, because we lose all muscle tone during REM sleep.) In the human ancestral environment, the main protection against predators was a close-knit social group. The human brain evolved under conditions that made this sense of social belonging and social connectedness the basis for feelings of relative safety. Natural tendencies in the human brain continue to reflect these links, so that fears of social rejection can evoke powerful feelings of threat and so lead to sleep disruption, while feelings of love, caring, and social connection create a feeling of safety and so promote sleep.

Finally, it is important to consider the ways in which the sleep and vigilance systems change during adolescent development. The maturation of humans during puberty includes physical and mental changes in preparation for taking on adult roles (with increased demands for threat appraisal and response). Changes in the vigilance system include a greater capacity for sleep disruptions from social stresses, including fears, anxieties, and emotional arousal.[2] Thus adolescent sleep systems appear to become more vulnerable to stress at a time when social turmoil and difficulties are often increasing.

Consequences of Insufficient Sleep in Adolescents

There is a surprising lack of controlled studies examining the effects of sleep deprivation or insufficient sleep among adolescents. However, there is extensive circumstantial evidence, clinical evidence, and research in adults that is relevant to these questions. While there is a general convergence of these findings, one important caveat is that we need a greater number of direct investigations. A second note of caution is that we lack information about *long-term* or *chronic* effects of insufficient sleep, since the limited data available have addressed only the immediate and short-term effects of sleep loss.

In brief, there are four main effects of acute sleep loss: 1) sleepiness, 2) motivational aspects of tiredness, 3) emotional changes, and 4) alterations in attention and performance. Before discussing each of these briefly, I wish to stress one general principle that applies across categories: the influence of *effort*. That is, the effects of sleep deprivation can be offset or even overridden for *short* periods of time by increased effort (or by increasing the external motivation to perform through rewards or punishments). The good news here is that most capabilities can be maintained over a short interval if necessary, while the bad news is that everything is harder to do. In some ways this is the cardinal feature of sleep deprivation: it takes increased effort to perform the same cognitive, emotional, or physical tasks.

1. *Sleepiness*. The most obvious and direct effect of inadequate sleep is a feeling of sleepiness. Sleepiness is most problematic during periods of low stimulation, such as in the classroom, when reading or driving, or when doing repetitive activities. Highly stimulating activities — particularly those involving physical activity or emotional arousal — can often mask moderate levels of sleepiness. Thus many sleep-deprived adolescents report that they can stay out very late at night and not feel tired, whereas if they were to lie quietly reading a book, they would fall asleep in minutes. (However, see the discussion of circadian influences in the article by Mary Carskadon, page 11.)

Another important aspect of sleepiness is the tendency toward brief mental lapses or microsleeps. Often, an individual is not even aware of these short gaps in awareness and responsiveness. However, such a lapse in the midst of driving, operating machinery, or doing anything else that requires vigilance can have dire consequences.

Several indirect consequences of sleepiness are also worth mentioning. These include adolescent conflicts with parents and teachers that arise from the difficulty of getting up in the morning or the ease of falling asleep in class; increased use of stimulants (particularly caffeine and nicotine); and synergistic effects with alcohol (the impairments from a combination of alcohol and sleepiness appear to be more than additive, resulting in a deadly combination of influences).

2. *Tiredness*. A separate symptom of sleep loss that can be defined as a feeling of fatigue or decreased motivation is tiredness. Tiredness makes it difficult to initiate (and persist at) certain types of behavior (especially tasks deemed boring or tedious). The effects of tiredness are less apparent when performing tasks that are naturally engaging, exciting, or threatening — perhaps because it is easier to recruit extra effort to offset tiredness. Conversely, the effects of tiredness are more pronounced for tasks

that require motivation to be derived from abstract goals or consequences (e.g., reading or studying uninteresting material in order to increase the chances of attaining some future reward).

Tedious tasks without the imminent prospect of reward (or fear of immediate consequences) are much more difficult to initiate and complete when one has been deprived of sleep. Similarly, tasks that require planning, strategy, or a complex sequence of steps to complete are more difficult when one is tired. This general category of tasks (requiring motivation linked to abstract goals, delayed rewards/consequences, planning, strategy, and so on) involves abstract processing areas in the front of the brain (regions of the prefrontal cortex) that appear to be particularly sensitive to sleep deprivation.[3] The potential relevance of these types of motivational changes to educational goals and processes seems obvious.

3. *Emotional changes.* The emotional changes that are secondary effects of sleep loss are very important but very complex. There are at least three factors that make this a complicated area for investigators: 1) the emotional effects of sleep deprivation appear to be highly variable across individuals and across situations, 2) emotion and emotional regulation are very hard to measure accurately, and 3) there are bi-directional interactions between mood and sleep disturbances (this third aspect was noted above and will be addressed separately below).

One of the main sources of information in this area comes from clinical descriptions of children and adolescents with various sorts of sleep disorders or transient sleep disruptions. There are also a few studies (including ongoing research in our laboratory) that obtain measures of emotion before, during, and after a single night of sleep deprivation, and then again following a recovery sleep.

The major theme across these studies is evidence suggesting *mood lability*. Not only does there appear to be greater variability in emotional states following sleep loss, but there also appears to be less control over emotional responses in many adolescents. For example, if faced with a frustrating task, a sleep-deprived teenager is more likely to become angry or aggressive. Yet, in response to something humorous, the same subject might act more silly or inane. Several adolescents reported increased crying reactions during sad scenes in videotaped movies when they were sleep-deprived. Many subjects reported increased irritability, impatience, and low tolerance for frustration when asked to perform tedious computer tasks. In general, these findings often looked like a decrease in inhibition or conscious control over emotions following sleep loss. It is also important to point out that some subjects seemed to show no measurable changes in any emotion when sleep-deprived.

These results are quite preliminary, include a high degree of variability across individuals, and will require replication with larger samples to establish statistical significance. However, these findings fit very well within a general pattern of similar observations regarding *effortful control*. That is, the primary emotional changes following sleep loss suggest a decrease in the ability to control, inhibit, or modify emotional responses to bring them into line with long-term goals, social rules, or other learned principles. Effortful control over emotion involves regions of the prefrontal cortex of the brain that are similar to those discussed previously with regard to abstract goals.

Changes in emotional regulation that result in decreased control following sleep loss could have serious consequences in terms of many high-risk behaviors among adolescents. The inability to control emotional responses could influence aggression, sexual behavior, the use of alcohol and drugs, and risky driving. Clearly, additional research will be needed to better delineate these complex but important issues relevant to adolescent health.

4. *Changes in attention and performance.* Following sleep loss, changes in attention and performance also represent a complex area of investigation in children and adolescents. There are three main points. First, sleep loss is associated with brief mental lapses in attention during simple tasks that can be partially offset by increased effort or motivation. Second, sleep deprivation can sometimes mimic or exacerbate symptoms of ADHD (attention deficit/hyperactivity disorder), including distractibility, impulsiv-

ity, and difficulty with effortful control of attention. Third, there is also emerging evidence that sleep deprivation has marked influences on the ability to perform complex tasks or tasks that require attention in two or more areas at the same time.

While the first point about brief mental lapses has already been addressed, the latter two points warrant some discussion. A potential link between ADHD symptoms and sleep deprivation has received considerable discussion from several investigators.[4] Both ADHD and sleep deprivation are associated with difficulty with self-control of behavior, attention, and impulses. Both ADHD and the daytime symptoms of sleep deprivation will often respond to stimulant medication. Furthermore, ADHD symptoms are more frequent in children with sleep disorders, and there has been some reported improvement in ADHD symptoms in children following treatment of sleep problems. Finally, other studies have reported increased rates of sleep complaints and disorders in children diagnosed with ADHD. This is a very complex area, and disentangling the connections and relative contributions across these domains will require additional careful studies.

One pragmatic recommendation, however, is quite simple. For any child or adolescent who exhibits symptoms of ADHD, the importance of a good night's sleep and a regular sleep/wake schedule should be emphasized to avoid the consequences of sleep loss that could exacerbate symptoms.

One of the most interesting areas of study is evidence that some types of complex tasks may be particularly sensitive to the effects of sleep deprivation. James Horne has presented extensive evidence showing that dual tasks and tasks that require creative or flexible thinking are sensitive to sleep loss.[5] (These tasks all require abstract processing in areas of the prefrontal cortex.) Our own research group has generated similar findings in its examination of dual tasks following sleep deprivation in adolescents and young adults. For example, students with one night of sleep deprivation exhibited no significant changes in performance on a difficult computer task and showed no effect on postural balance. However, when the students performed both tasks simultaneously, sleep deprivation had a marked effect on balance.[6] In recent pilot studies we have also found the same pattern of results in adolescents performing cognitive and emotional tasks. Performance at either task could be maintained following sleep deprivation — but not both.

On one hand, detriments in performing a dual task (like controlling thoughts and feelings at the same time) might sound like an esoteric or subtle effect of sleep deprivation; on the other hand, it is important to point out that fluency in such dual tasks is the foundation of social competence. These are the daily challenges that must be balanced in the everyday life of adolescents: thinking and solving problems while navigating the emotional reactions of complex social situations, using self-control over impulses and emotions while pursuing goals, experiencing anger yet weighing the long-term consequences of actions. If further research substantiates the marked effects of insufficient sleep on these types of complex tasks in adolescents, then we should have significant concerns about the importance of sleep patterns in the normal development of social competence.

Sleep and Emotional Disorders in Adolescents

It is essential to underscore the complex intersection between sleep regulation and behavioral and emotional problems in adolescents. Clearly, there are two-way interactions between these systems. The regulation and timing of sleep can be altered by behavioral or emotional disorders, while cognitive, behavioral, and emotional control during daytime hours can be influenced by the way adolescents sleep. Furthermore, daytime activities, changes in the environment, and stressful events can have profound transient effects on sleeping patterns in the absence of any clear-cut psychopathology. In addition, medications used to treat psychiatric disorders often affect sleep, and sleep loss can exacerbate mood and behavioral symptoms.

Perhaps the best-studied example of such interactions is the relationship between sleep and depression. Subjective sleep complaints are very common in children and adolescents who have been diagnosed with Major Depressive Disorder (MDD). Symptoms include insomnia (75% of cases) and hypersomnia (25%). Hypersomnia difficulties are reported more frequently after puberty. Insomnia symptoms usually include difficulty falling asleep and a subjective sense of not having slept deeply all night.

Recently, clinicians and researchers have seen increasing numbers of adolescents with overlapping phase delay disorders or other sleep/wake schedule disorders associated with depression. Depressed adolescents frequently have difficulty falling asleep, are unable to get up or refuse to go to school, sleep until late in the day, complain of extreme daytime fatigue, and, over time, shift to increasingly more delayed sleep/wake schedules. Likewise, surveys reveal that adolescents who get less than 6¾ hours of sleep each school night or report more than a two-hour difference between school night and weekend bedtimes have a higher level of complaints of depressed mood than adolescents who get more sleep or who sleep on more regular sleep/wake schedules.

Clinicians who are experienced with these problems have pointed out that in many cases it is difficult to differentiate decreased motivation, school refusal/anxiety, delayed circadian phase, attention difficulties, and depressive symptomatology. Clearly, both sleep patterns and behavioral symptoms must be carefully assessed in an effort to prevent the problems, diagnose them accurately, and plan successful treatment.

There is also evidence of changes in the sleeping electroencephalograms (EEGs) of depressed adolescents, including increased time to fall asleep and altered patterns of REM sleep. Furthermore, changes in EEG measures of sleep predicted an increased recurrence of depressive episodes during longitudinal follow-ups in early adulthood.[7]

In some cases, treatment of sleep complaints and problems — including regularizing the sleep/wake schedule, cognitive behavioral therapy for insomnia, and short-term treatment with medication for severe insomnia — can have a positive impact on depressive symptoms.[8] On the other hand, effective treatment of depression can also be a critical aspect of improving sleep.

Negative Spirals?

As I described above, one area of concern with regard to the interconnections between sleep and emotional disturbances is the potential for a progressive sequence or spiral of negative effects. Insufficient sleep can amplify emotional difficulties, which can then produce further sources of distress and increased disruption of sleep. The reason for this concern arises more from clinical experience than from any controlled studies, and so the concern is perhaps best illustrated by describing a case.

Jay had a history of poor sleep habits (e.g., bedtimes past midnight, erratic sleep/wake schedule) beginning in about seventh grade. In ninth grade the problems became worse as he struggled to get to sleep at night (usually falling asleep at 1 a.m.) and to wake up in the morning and then had problems with distractibility and behavior at school. He also reported some symptoms of depression, including loss of interest in some activities, daytime fatigue, and worsening performance at school. His symptoms improved transiently in the summer, when he slept from 3 a.m. until noon.

In 10th grade Jay began attending a high school that started at 7:30 a.m., which required him to wake up at 6 a.m. to meet the school bus at 6:30 a.m. He had a very difficult time getting up for school at that hour because his average bedtime was 2 a.m. He made several attempts to go to bed earlier but found himself unable to fall asleep. He was never able to follow through in a way that would permit him to establish an earlier pattern of bedtime, and he quickly reverted to his 3 a.m.-to-noon sleep schedule on all weekends and holidays. Jay sometimes stayed up working at his computer or watching television — he says this was because he hated the feeling of lying in bed trying unsuccessfully to fall asleep. Before long, he was regularly missing school or arriving late and falling asleep in class.

Jay, who had at one time been identified as a gifted student, was failing most of his classes and appeared increasingly lethargic, subdued, and uninterested in school. His school counselor referred him to a mental health clinic. Over the course of several months, he was diagnosed as having depression with some ADHD symptoms (e.g., difficulty finishing tasks, distractibility). Trials of antidepressants and stimulant medication resulted in small transient improvements in some symptoms, but Jay was never able to reestablish good sleep patterns that were compatible with his school schedule. Eventually he withdrew from school, became increasingly depressed and withdrawn, and was hospitalized after a serious suicide attempt.

At the time of hospitalization, Jay had severe chronic insomnia and a major depressive disorder. Despite multiple interventions, these problems persisted. He showed very little motivation to return to school and appeared to have chronic depressive symptoms. At discharge his long-term prognosis was not promising.

In a case such as Jay's, it is impossible to disentangle the relative contributions of the sleep and mood dysregulations. While no general conclusions can be drawn from this single case, it does illustrate the complexity of these interactions and the importance of obtaining a better understanding in these areas.

Policy Decisions for Today and Direction for the Future

Frequently in this article I have cautioned readers about the need for additional research to improve our understanding of the complex issues arising from the consequences of insufficient sleep among adolescents. Our current knowledge is preliminary and based on a paucity of controlled data. Furthermore, we are probably at an equally early stage in our understanding of the behavioral and emotional problems of adolescents.

Nonetheless, behavioral and emotional difficulties are currently the largest source of morbidity and mortality among adolescents. While it is possible that sleep loss makes only a minuscule contribution to adolescents' problems with emotional regulation, it is extremely likely that it plays some role. It is also quite possible that insufficient sleep plays a significant role in leading up to some of these problems in a vulnerable set of individuals.

Identifying vulnerability to sleep loss may represent an important future direction for research, since there appear to be such large individual differences in the effects of acute sleep loss. Such vulnerability could be related to a tendency to need more sleep, to being a "night owl," or to a biological vulnerability toward emotional disorders.

Clearly, more research is needed to help inform policy makers, whose decisions will further affect adolescent sleep patterns. Cost-benefit analyses regarding the relative importance of sleep will require more precise quantification in these areas. In the meantime, one might make a reasonable case that the odds are heavily in favor of sleep as an increasingly important health concern among adolescents.

To reiterate the main point with which I began, adequate sleep is defined as the amount necessary for optimal daytime functioning. It appears that the potentially fragile underpinnings of adolescent social competence (controlling thoughts and feelings at the same time) may be most sensitive to the effects of inadequate sleep. Any review of adolescent lifestyles in our society will reveal more than a dozen forces converging to push the sleep/arousal balance away from sleep and toward ever-higher arousal. What harm could there be in trying to push back a little toward valuing sleep? The potential benefits seem enormous.

Notes

1. Ronald E. Dahl, "The Regulation of Sleep and Arousal: Development and Psychopathology," *Development and Psychopathology*, vol. 8, 1996, pp. 3-27.
2. Ronald E. Dahl et al., "Sleep Onset Abnormalities in Depressed Adolescents," *Biological Psychiatry*, vol. 39, 1996, pp. 400-10.
3. James A. Horne, "Human Sleep, Sleep Loss, and Behaviour Implications for the Prefrontal Cortex and Psychiatric Disorder," *British Journal of Psychiatry*, vol. 162, 1993, pp. 413-19.
4. Ronald D. Chervin et al., "Symptoms of Sleep Disorders, Inattention, and Hyperactivity in Children," *Sleep*, vol. 20, 1997, pp. 1185-92.

5. Horne, op. cit.
6. Abigail Schlesinger, Mark S. Redfern, Ronald E. Dahl, and J. Richard Jennings, "Postural Control, Attention and Sleep Deprivation," *Neuroreport*, vol. 9, 1998, pp. 49-52.
7. Uma Rao et al., "The Relationship Between Longitudinal Clinical Course and Sleep and Cortisol Changes in Adolescent Depression," *Biological Psychiatry*, vol. 40, 1996, pp. 474-84.
8. Ronald E. Dahl, "Child and Adolescent Sleep Disorders," in idem, ed., *Child and Adolescent Psychiatric Clinics of North America: Sleep Disorder* (Philadelphia: W.B. Saunders, 1996).

The Impact of
School Starting Time
on Family Life

GORDON D. WROBEL

Gordon D. Wrobel is a nationally certified school psychologist and licensed psychologist whose professional focus has been children and youths with emotional and behavioral disorders. He is a doctoral candidate in educational psychology at the University of Minnesota, Minneapolis.

When asked, most parents can provide vivid descriptions of what they believe to be a cause-and-effect relationship between their child's disrupted sleep and subsequent deficits in mood, behavior, and performance. Even young children can readily report a clear connection between their sleep and how they feel, relate to others, and meet the challenges of the day.

Despite a common awareness of the importance of sleep, little formal study has been done to document factors affecting the reciprocal relationship between sleep and the family milieu. The Center for Applied Research and Educational Improvement (CAREI) at the University of Minnesota has been engaged in two studies (referred to here collectively as "the CAREI study") that are attempting to examine the impact of changes in school starting times across the school, community, and family contexts. While not initially a primary focus of the CAREI study, the impact that changing school starting times has on families has emerged as an important factor deserving of more careful examination.

Why Sleep Is Important to Education Policy

While there is a growing medical literature investigating the effects of sleep on the health and performance of children and youths, there has been little crossover between the fields of sleep medicine and primary and secondary education.[1] Consequently, education policy makers have not typically considered sleep as an important factor affecting the educational process. This fact is remarkable, given the substantiated connection between sleep and educational performance.[2]

According to Ronald Dahl, "There are very few data on sleep deprivation in normal children."[3] Despite the lack of data, there is a growing concern that children, and especially adolescents, are not getting the sleep they require to be at their best in school, at work, or in the community.[4] Some school districts that have been alerted to this concern have responded by changing to a later school starting time for adolescents. Education policy makers have sometimes forged ahead with sweeping changes in school starting times without the benefit of well-thought-out plans for policy development and implementation.[5] The current CAREI study suggests that there are but a handful of formal studies that examine the actual impact of changes in school starting time on student learning and behavior.

In addition, CAREI has found no study of sleep that has focused on the family milieu and how it affects and is affected by changes in school starting time. Yet common experience tells us that the family context plays a critical role in how students present themselves at school. Preliminary results of the CAREI study suggest that changes in school starting time can and do have a profound effect on families. The impact has been reported in nearly all facets of family life: school, work, leisure time, and even family traditions. There appears to be a rather complex interaction between the family milieu and changes in school starting time. Clearly, not all families are affected by such schedule changes in the same way or to the same degree. For some families a change in school starting time results in dramatic positive changes, while the same change for another family may be devastating.

The Impact on the Family

It should be remembered that the family context was not a primary focus of the CAREI study. Concerns relative to the family emerged from the research process and the data. Consequently, the impressions developed here should be seen only as a guide for further formal study. Nevertheless, the dramatic reports that surfaced suggest that education policy makers and communities may benefit from considering the impact that schedule changes will have on families.

The study of sleep necessitates an examination of the family context, if for no other reason than that the home is where the event of interest — sleep — most frequently occurs. The family milieu presents a number of challenges for the researcher. Key variables such as the quantity and quality of sleep are difficult to control. Parents are typically reluctant to volunteer their children for research, regardless of the nature of the study. In addition, children are particularly resistant to sleeping outside of their homes, which often eliminates the opportunity for controlled observation of a subject's sleep. Children and youths often have privacy concerns relative to the self-reporting of the details of their sleep, such as what time they go to bed and the quality of their sleep. It has also been our experience that many children and youths have a difficult time accurately maintaining even simple records of sleep patterns. In addition, parents have been shown to be particularly poor reporters of their children's sleep habits. Taken as a whole, these complications can compromise even the best-planned research design, especially when attempting to relate sleep to measures of daytime performance.

47

Because of the complications of obtaining accurate data regarding sleep and wake patterns of children and youths, CAREI developed a research design that used multiple data sources in an effort to begin to examine the relationship between sleep and daytime student performance. The current study has four primary data sources: 1) focus group interviews with students, parents, and school staff members; 2) a School Sleep Habits Survey completed by students; 3) telephone interviews with parents and key stakeholders; and 4) written surveys of teachers.

Some 18 urban and suburban school districts have been involved in the CAREI study. Over 10,000 participants have included students, parents, school staff members, and key stakeholders in the community. In addition to the self-report data offered by students and parents, school staff members were asked to comment on what they had heard from parents. Staff members who were also parents offered their own parental experiences as well.

Two overarching themes emerged from this data set. First, the impact of changing school starting time is profound for many families. Families experience a wide range of positive and negative effects when the school schedule changes. While some families reported little difficulty in adjusting to the new schedule, others were devastated by the stress of attempting to meet the new demands on their time. Even those families who reported having little difficulty adjusting to the schedule changes saw both advantages and disadvantages to the change in school starting time.

Second, how the policy process played out in each community had a substantial impact on how the changes were received by families. Some school districts and individual schools took great pains to involve the school community and keep members informed of the anticipated changes in school starting time. Other districts and schools had as little as one week to implement the change in schedule. Clearly, those districts and school communities that had ample warning reported less difficulty in making the necessary adjustments. As one elementary school principal recalled, "We did work up front involving the community. Talking about it. Talking to our staff and having the staff vote on when they wanted to start. Do they want their meetings on the front end or the back end of the school day? And it happened. There was a lot of preparation."

The CAREI study found that students and parents were keenly aware of the policy process. How these stakeholders perceived their involvement in the process affected how they responded to the changes. Those who described the policy process as open and sensitive to their needs reported being better able to make informed decisions about which school to attend, which schedule options to choose, and how best to meet their needs. Those families that reported feeling devalued in the process were often vocal in their distrust of the justifications offered for making the schedule change. One parent told us, "I was in agreement with the change because I had been able to read the literature. But I also know that staff and students were very cynical about how the decision was made. And there was a lot of feeling that people were not consulted or talked to and it was just decided."

Most of the schools in this study were engaged in a number of significant change initiatives, which made it difficult to sort out the impact of the change in starting time from all the other influences. For example, some schools had implemented a school attendance program independent of the change in starting time. Despite this, participants in the CAREI study readily offered opinions about the impact of school schedule on school attendance. Another factor that made it more difficult to assess the effects of changes in school starting time was that most of the schools involved in the study did not begin collecting relevant data until after the changes had been made.

Economics as a Factor in Starting Time Policy

The impact of changing school starting time was not the same for all communities in the CAREI study. The concerns expressed about the changes were clearly related to the relative affluence of school communities. For example, transportation to and from school and other activities was a substantial, if not primary, concern in the less affluent school districts, where viable alternatives to school transportation were typically reported to be limited or nonexistent. As one parent told us, "My children miss more school. I don't have a car. The bus is there so early, and if they're late, they miss it, and I can't get them to school."

The more affluent districts consistently reported that their primary concern in designing a school schedule was the best interests of students. Students, parents, and staff members from less affluent schools consistently reported that they thought that administrators considered the best interests of students to be secondary to the realities of the transportation budget. This attitude, when combined with a problematic policy process, fostered an atmosphere of mistrust of — and, in some cases, open anger with — the school administration. "It is unfortunate that the scheduling of buses dictates the schedule for school," one parent remarked. "The central office doesn't base any of its decisions on what parents or students want in this district. They are basing the decision solely on what's cheaper to run as far as transportation costs," complained another. In such situations it was difficult to segregate fundamental concerns about disrespect and disenfranchisement from concerns related to the change in school starting time.

A clear relationship emerged between economics and the ability to adjust to the time change. Families with ample resources tended to be actively involved in creating and taking advantage of alternative means of meeting new schedule demands. Families with limited resources saw themselves as having few options and often reported being overwhelmed by the same demands. Affluent parents talked of needing to adjust their work schedules in order to support their children's school and activity schedules. Parents with limited resources talked of the stress associated with having to change jobs because their current jobs did not offer the kind of flexibility they needed in order to meet their children's schedule. Day care and supervision of their children also presented major concerns and challenges.

The change in school schedule had an impact on the number of transitions young students experienced each day. Students might have to go from home to day care, come home after school to an empty house, or wait alone in the school building for long periods. These transitional periods of the day often had little organized activity, and it was difficult for children to use these times to do homework. Some parents were now burdened with the need to provide both morning and evening child care. For other parents and their children, however, the new schedule meant fewer transitions and an increase in quality family time. One parent reported, "I've been fortunate. My mother works in my son's school district. I take him to her house for breakfast, and they walk to school together. If that hadn't been the case, it would have been awful to have to put him in day care both before and after school."

In order to maintain their jobs, some parents whose work schedule did not match their children's school schedule had to leave their children unsupervised for parts of the day. These parents were clearly troubled by the situation and often reported seeing no other alternative. Many of these parents mentioned that affordable, reliable day-care options simply did not exist in their community. Others stated that older siblings who had previously provided interim supervision for younger siblings were now unavailable because of the later end to the older siblings' school day. In these communities, students, parents, and school staff members alike reported significant concern over the amount of time that young children were being left unsupervised. This concern did not surface in the more affluent districts.

Some students' families expected them to work, either to supplement the basic family income or to cover unmet personal expenses and leisure activities. Because labor laws limit the time of day that youths can work, changes to a later ending time for school often meant that fewer hours were available for students to work. Students reported not only that there were fewer hours but also that late arrivers were often relegated to the least desirable job duties, such as cleanup and closing activities.

Family and Community Norms

While the CAREI study did not focus on community, family, and cultural differences, it became clear that there were norms with regard to time that created expectations about what is appropriate behavior. These attitudes were often based on individuals' personal experiences and did not acknowledge that there is a spectrum of needs relative to the amount and scheduling of sleep. As an example, persons who were raised in an agricultural setting, where early waking schedules were the norm, saw early starting times for school as not only normal but preferred and valued. People who were late risers were seen as lazy and unmotivated. In focus group interviews, an "owl's" disclosure of a preference for a later schedule often brought deprecatory comments and laughter from the others in the group.

Consistent across all schools were the complaints by parents and students that there were simply too many demands on their time. Some communities expected their children to be involved in numerous extracurricular and volunteer activities. Many students mentioned having virtually no personal time to unwind or relax and reported experiencing deleterious effects from excessive commitments and time demands. It was not uncommon for students to refer to extreme fatigue and associated health problems. For the most part, students were making the choices to be committed to these activities, but in some instances, pressure came from the student's social milieu.

Students commonly reported the perception that success as an adult was directly related to overextending themselves with activities while in high school. One student told us, "There's a lot of times I'm sitting in school and I'm saying, 'Geez, I just want to go home,' and then I realize I get to step off my bus, put on my work shirt, and run to my work because I've got to be down there." Another student complained, "Since I like to do a lot of stuff after school, the later starting time conflicts with that. I get home late, and I want to do stuff after school. The school district thinks that you have just as much time because you can stay up later. But after 9 or 10 p.m. for me, it doesn't feel right to do homework anymore. So that just really limits my time, and it limits what I can do because I get home so late."

It was apparent when looking at the data across communities that not all schools were equally supported in making the schedule changes. Some communities expended substantial effort to ensure that schedules for before- and after-school activities were accommodating. In other communities, respondents told us that the school schedule was the only one to change and that they felt out of synch with the rest of the world. The conflicting schedules affected opportunities for recreation and sports, medical appointments, and jobs for teens.

One teacher noted, "When these starting times were changed, many people, especially school administrators in our district, asked, 'What is going to happen with regard to the community and the theater and sports?' And the answer we were given was, 'The rest of the world will adjust to accommodate us.' But no one has adjusted to accommodate us. Our transportation department hasn't even accommodated us. We can only schedule field trips during certain hours of the day." Said another, "Nothing meshes as well as it should. The learning doesn't mesh; the social skills that go on the rest of the day, they just don't mesh; my family life doesn't mesh; everything is off. So that affects my attitude and affects the kids' attitudes and their abilities in school."

One could easily be led to believe that the best possible school schedule would be the one that would most closely match the schedule of the family. Certainly the family routine is of great importance. Yet simply matching a family's schedule may not be in the best educational interests of the students. It is clear from our findings that families differ substantially in their ability to adjust to schedule demands and changes. Participants readily identified themselves and their children as "morning" or "evening" people. They were quick to point out preferred personal schedules and the problems associated with mismatches between time demands and natural rhythms.

Impact on Students

The student participants in the CAREI study were generally very aware of policy discussions regarding school starting time. Some schools had gone to great lengths to inform and involve students in the decision process. Some students reported having discussed the impact of sleep on student performance as part of their school's curriculum. In those schools, it was not uncommon to hear students quote research they had read or to relate discussions they had had with their peers and teachers. Students were aware that sleep plays an important role in their school performance. These students had been empowered to make informed decisions about their sleep habits, and they often articulated concern about the difficult decisions they needed to make regarding time management.

In schools where student involvement in the policy process was limited, it was commonly reported that students simply stayed up later as a result of the later starting time. It was their perception that changing the starting time had little impact on the total sleep students were getting. Many reported that they and their peers were filling their available time with more late-night television viewing. School staff members also reported a concern that even young children were now staying up late to watch adult-oriented programs.

One might be inclined to generalize that all young people would opt for the later starting time if given the opportunity. We did not find this to be the case. Many students who experienced a change to a later start reported a desire to have an earlier starting time. For these students the earlier time was seen to be a better match for their natural schedules or to provide more opportunity to participate in activities after school. Many students reported that they enjoyed getting up early in order to be done with their school day early. The early end to the school day left ample time for after-school activities, work, and socializing.

An unanticipated problem that school staff members reported was that many of the elementary students on the late schedule had viewed as much as two or three hours of television in the morning before coming to school. This programming, largely cartoons, often contained violent themes that were replayed in the classroom, much to the dismay of the teacher.

For some elementary students, a late school start necessitated an early morning day-care transition. Staff members felt that this was hard on many of the students and left them fatigued at the end of the day. In addition, elementary school staff members reported that the prime learning time for this age group is in the morning and that later schedules afford less of this optimum time.

Students with special needs, while not a focus of this study, were often mentioned as being affected differently from the general school population. Parents with children who had substantial needs for personal care reported significant advantages to later starts. Students with emotional and behavioral concerns were seen to be particularly affected by changes in school starting time. The behavior of this group of students tended to deteriorate in the afternoons, which suggested that earlier starting times were preferable to later starts. Further study with this group of students may provide important insights into the relationship between sleep and daytime behavioral functioning.

Other Considerations

Ethnic and cultural variables were not specifically examined in this study. However, concerns were raised about how students from various cultural and ethnic backgrounds might have been differentially affected by the change in school starting time. For example, it was reported that students who fasted as a religious custom often had difficulty maintaining their fasts because of either an early starting time or a late dismissal time.

While the intention of moving to a later starting time for adolescents was to increase the available time for sleep, some students actually found that they had less time to sleep because of time demands within the family. A host of reports suggested that some family schedules did not change to accommodate the changes in the school schedule. Some families have traditions requiring adolescents to assist with meal preparation, child care, and other household duties. Students in these families still needed to get up early to complete their family duties, even though they were required to remain in school until later in the day. For these students there was a net loss of time available for activities and sleep.

For other families, the change in school starting time meant that the family schedule was now more in synch. Parents and children in these families reported having more quality time together. They now had time to prepare for the day together, eat meals together, and enjoy a family activity after school because of the lack of conflicting commitments in their respective schedules. Yet other parents and students reported that the same changes in the school schedule resulted in lost opportunities to be together as a family.

Students, parents, and school staff members all mentioned concerns regarding certain school schedules and nutrition. Schedules that demanded that mealtimes be at odd hours were seen to put some students at a disadvantage. Students of all ages complained of hunger that kept them from concentrating on their work or doing their best. Teachers talked about needing to provide snacks to older elementary students to accommodate their hunger.

Several parents commented that they had noticed differences in their children's attitude toward school as a result of the change in starting time. Interactions between parents and children were strained when parents had to struggle to get their children to comply with a newly implemented early start. These struggles set in place a negative attitude for the student, which was often carried over into the school day. Seemingly insignificant concerns, such as access to the bathroom in the morning, took on greater significance in homes where children and parents were feeling rushed. Several parents reported having observed a decline in their children's attitude toward school in general as a result of the need to be up early.

Parents whose children attended schools starting later reported fewer behavioral concerns and an improved attitude toward school. "The change to a later school starting time has made for a happier family," noted one. "The kids are more rested, and there is less fighting in the house."

Other parents suggested that the changes had little impact. They simply adjusted their schedules to provide ample time for sleep and morning preparation. In fact, several stated that the process of adapting to the change in school starting time provided a valuable learning experience for their children. One parent reported, "Our children were pretty disciplined. They went to bed earlier to get up earlier. It was a bit awkward with the extra time in the morning. It taught them how to use their time."

Guidelines for Family-Friendly Policies

The following guidelines are meant to aid policy makers in developing and implementing changes in school starting time. These suggestions are based on the experience of schools participating in the CAREI study and pertain particularly to the aspects of the process that will involve families and help them make the needed changes in their family routines.

1. *Inform and involve all stakeholders.* This suggestion may seem all too obvious. However, policy makers need to understand that changes in school starting time affect virtually every aspect of family and community life. The sooner stakeholders are involved in the decision, the sooner problems can be anticipated, adaptations created, and solutions implemented.

2. *Allow ample time.* A significant change in a family's schedule will take time to arrange. A year of planning before the implementation of changes in school starting time would not be unreasonable. Adequate time will allow stakeholders to become informed and to make reasoned decisions about what is best for their situation.

3. *Provide justifications for decisions based on research data.* Families and students will use information if it is made available. Families want to know that changes are being made in the best interests of their children. They want to be able to weigh the decisions and have alternatives defined.

4. *Support families in the decision process.* If your goal is to have students and families make good decisions about their schedules, understand that some may need to be supported in the process. This may require multiple methods of delivering information and will certainly demand culturally sensitive approaches to providing assistance. A change in school starting time may

well intrude on the customs of the family and, as such, could serve to alienate families from the school.

5. *Involve the community.* Thought should be given to who in the community will be affected by a change in starting time. Community members and agencies that can assist with the change should be enlisted. Examples would be churches, park boards, police, field trip sites, and employers.

6. *Don't forget the school staff.* Changes in starting time will affect school staff members, many of whom are also parents. Staff members need to be given options and ample time to make decisions about their personal and professional lives.

7. *Commit to providing follow-up regarding the change.* As the process moves forward, difficulties will continue to surface. Ultimately, changes in school starting time will probably have an effect on educational outcomes. It would be wise to monitor the impact of the changes so that the best interests of students remain a priority.

Notes

1. Millicent Lawton, "Too Little, Too Late," *Education Week*, 11 October 1995, pp. 33-35; and William C. Dement, "History of Sleep Physiology and Medicine," in Meir H. Kryger, Thomas Roth, and William C. Dement, eds., *Principles and Practice of Sleep Medicine*, 2nd ed. (Philadelphia: W.B. Saunders, 1994), pp. 3-15.
2. Kyla L. Wahlstrom and Carol M. Freeman, *School Start Time Study: Preliminary Report of Findings* (Minneapolis: Center for Applied Research and Educational Improvement, University of Minnesota, 1997); and Joel Frederickson and Gordon D. Wrobel, *School Start Time Study: Technical Report, Vol. II* (Minneapolis: Center for Applied Research and Educational Improvement, University of Minnesota, 1997).
3. Ronald E. Dahl, "The Regulation of Sleep and Arousal: Development and Psychopathology," *Development and Psychopathology*, vol. 8, 1996, p. 9.
4. Mary A. Carskadon, "Patterns of Sleep and Sleepiness in Adolescents," *Pediatrician*, vol. 17, 1990, pp. 5-12.

5. Kyla Wahlstrom, Gordon Wrobel, and Patricia Kubo
   Summary of Findings from Minneapolis School Di:
   Start Time Study," 1998, available from http://carei.col£

Starting Time and School Life: Reflections from Educators and Students

PATRICIA K. KUBOW
KYLA L. WAHLSTROM
AMY E. BEMIS

Patricia K. Kubow *is an assistant professor at Bowling Green State University, Bowling Green, Ohio. Kyla L. Wahlstrom is associate director of the Center for Applied Research and Educational Improvement, University of Minnesota, Minneapolis, where Amy E. Bemis is an education specialist.*

With the 1997-98 school year in the Minneapolis Public Schools (MPS) came a change in the starting time for most of the schools in the district. It appears that Minneapolis may be the first major metropolitan school district in the United States to undertake systemwide changes in school starting time based on the current research about adolescents and their sleep needs. The seven high schools changed from a 7:15 a.m. to an 8:40 a.m. start; the seven middle schools moved from 7:40 to 9:40; and the starting times for the 71 elementary schools were set at either 7:40, 8:40, or 9:40.

A study is being conducted by the Center for Applied Research and Educational Improvement (CAREI) at the University of Minnesota in conjunction with the MPS to ascertain the impact of changing school starting times on the educational endeavor and on the community. The findings reveal that the changes affect the various stakeholders differently and are acutely felt at the personal level.

Methodology

The data were collected through the use of a written teacher survey and focus groups. The focus groups were held first because the issues of the various stakeholder groups were extremely diverse and needed clarification before a questionnaire could be developed. Secondary and elementary schools were drawn from a stratified random sample of schools in order to identify participants for the focus groups. Groups were conducted separately with teachers, students, and support/administrative staff members at three high schools and five middle schools. Administrators from each school solicited volunteers and ensured that each grade level was represented. While not specifically controlled for in this study, informal attempts were made to generate a diverse group of participants in terms of gender, ethnicity, and opinion concerning the starting time. Focus groups were also conducted at 14 elementary schools with only teachers and administrative/support staff members. In total, the 54 focus groups provided a forum for participants to reflect on the impact of the starting time changes and to identify areas of greatest concern.

The second form of data collection was a written survey for high school teachers developed from the findings of the MPS focus groups and from what was discovered during a case study of the Edina school district during the 1996-97 school year, reported in a larger study by Kyla Wahlstrom and Carol Freeman.[1] The one-page questionnaire comprised 12 Likert-style questions and three open-ended questions. A five-point scale was used as the response set for the quantitative questions. The survey was mailed to the homes of every Minneapolis high school teacher (n=568) after the end of the 1997-98 school year. The response rate was 67%. The survey was used to validate the focus group findings and was a means by which to have much broader teacher input than the use of focus groups could allow.

Findings from the High Schools

The focus group data from the high schools revealed that there were three main areas of concern regarding the change in starting time: its impact on students, its impact on teachers' instructional endeavors, and its impact on teachers' personal lives. Thus we developed a survey questionnaire that sought to gauge the magnitude of concern among teachers about those three areas.

Impact on students as perceived by teachers. Fifty-seven percent of the teachers responding to the written survey reported that a greater number of students were more alert during the first two periods of the day than had been the case with the earlier starting time. In fact, this item generated the most agreement of any question on the survey. Sixteen percent were neutral in their answers, and 27% disagreed. Slightly more than half (51%) of the teachers also agreed or strongly agreed that they saw fewer students sleeping at their desks. Interestingly, the respondents were evenly divided (33% agreed or strongly agreed, 32% neither agreed nor disagreed, 35% disagreed or strongly disagreed) regarding the statement "I see improved student behavior in general." This finding contrasts with the findings from Edina that reported markedly improved student behavior, as evidenced by quieter behavior in the hallways between classes and less lunchroom misbehavior.

Teachers were evenly divided in reporting the nature of the comments (positive versus negative) they had heard from students and from parents regarding the later starting time. Twenty-five percent said that they had heard neither positive nor negative comments from students, and 40% said that no comment had been heard from parents. Although practices, extended-day programs, and rehearsals were shortened, students still arrived home at a later hour than they had the previous year, fostering parental concerns about safety and somewhat reducing student participation in after-school activities.

Difficulties with students' work schedules were noted by several MPS respondents, who wrote that these teenagers had less time to work or had to work later in the day in order to put in as many hours as they once had. In the study by Wahlstrom and Freeman, 15 employers of suburban high school students were asked about the impact of the later start on their businesses. Fourteen of the 15 employers agreed that there had been no negative impact from the later dismissal, because their businesses did not need the extra help until the schools were dismissed. Minneapolis teachers observed that there appeared to be less involvement in extracurricular activities; Edina teachers did not notice any appreciable decrease in student involvement in after-school activities. Finally, both suburban and city teachers noted that some students seemed more tired at the end of the day, now that class extended an hour later into the afternoon. Additional parent feedback will be gathered in order to more fully understand the impact of the later start on students and families.

Impact on students as reported by students. Minneapolis high school students in the focus groups reported general dissatisfaction with the later start's impact on after-school activities and their own schedules. The data suggest some differentiation between grade levels, with ninth-graders consistently more negative about the later start than older students. Because the after-school schedule was pushed later in the day, students reported that they were more tired, had less time to study and do homework, and had shorter practices or practices at odd hours. For example, a lack of facilities and field lights necessitated morning practices; consequently, some students had to forgo the morning sleep that was to be a benefit of the later school starting time. Moreover, there were often conflicts in the scheduling of activities, forcing students to make tough decisions about which activity to choose and reducing their opportunities to participate in more than one.

As did the high school staff members, students expressed concern about having to leave school during the last period to attend practices and games and about middle-schoolers' being unable to participate in senior high athletics. Students explained that the later school starting time sometimes limited the number of hours they could work, reduced their income, and affected the types of jobs available to them. The schedule changes affected not only work, sports, and studying but also opportunities for relaxation and socialization. The good news is that several students reported that they were more alert and efficient during the day, and this enabled them to complete more of their homework at school.

Student focus groups in the suburban high school revealed a very different, and generally positive, picture. As in Minneapolis, some students mentioned that athletic practices were moved to an early morning time, which seemed to them to negate the beneficial effects of having a later start. However, the majority of students in the suburban focus groups said that they felt less tired at the end of the day when they did their homework and that the later dismissal had not negatively affected their involvement in after-school activities. Nearly all the students in the focus groups noted that they were feeling more rested and alert for the first hour of class and that they were generally going to bed at the same time as they had been when the starting time was an hour earlier — thus they were, indeed, getting about one hour more of sleep each school night.

Impact on instructional endeavors. By a slight majority, teachers reported that the later start enabled students to come to school more rested and therefore more ready for learning. The tradeoff, however, was that at the end of the day many student athletes needed to be excused from their last hour of class to get to an athletic event on time. One teacher wrote, "Now, I lose one-half of my sixth-hour International Baccalaureate class in the fall to sports' start times." The dilemma was felt by the coaches as well as the classroom teachers: "As a teacher and a coach, I was extremely troubled that I had to excuse my student athletes from class 13 times this spring for track meets. Many of us coaches were very distressed about this situation because it goes against everything we stand for as educators." The majority sentiment about students' missing class because of sports was summed up in this comment: "Please keep in mind that the primary purpose of schools is to educate, not to run extracurricular sports programs. The coaches will have to adapt." Clearly, this is a critical issue to resolve if the later starting time is to remain in place and benefit *all* students, not just those who are *not* involved in athletics.

During the focus groups with teachers, the participants noted that fewer students were seeking academic help before and after school. This concern was substantiated by the written survey, in which 50% of the teachers disagreed or strongly disagreed that more students were seeking academic help *before* school and 60% disagreed or strongly disagreed that more students were seeking academic help *after* school. Again, this was in direct contrast to the finding in Edina, where teachers reported that with the later start many more students came to school early to get additional help from teachers with their homework or to prepare for a quiz. Whether these findings are related to economics and having access to a car instead of having to rely on a school bus needs to be studied further.

During the focus groups, the high school teachers generally agreed that the 8:40 start had a negative impact on the end of the school day, defined as the time period right after lunch through the last academic hour. Because of early dismissals for activities, sports practices, and personal appointments, many students missed the last period. As a result, teachers were unable to cover the desired amount of curriculum, and students missed class discussions, labs, and required assignments. Some students even chose electives rather than required courses because they had to miss their last class so often. This, in turn, created a high demand for certain classes during fifth hour and small classes during sixth hour.

The impact of the late starting time on transportation issues and on learning appeared to be vastly different between the city high schools and the suburban high school. Being in the "second tier" of the MSP's three-tiered busing schedule meant that buses arrived late much more often. This was usually because of delays that occurred during the first run for the elementary schools that started at 7:40. One teacher noted, "Tardies are still a problem with the 8:40 start time, with many students late because of late buses. This is very frustrating — almost impossible to teach when you have a continuous stream of late students." Late buses were never mentioned by teachers as an ongoing problem in the suburban district of Edina, whose high school is also in the second tier of a three-tiered transportation schedule. However, it is very important to note that the suburb is about one-seventh the size of the city in terms of square miles, and it was easier to make up time with shorter distances between neighborhoods and schools.

Finally, many teachers in the high schools with a later starting time commented on the positive effect the change had had on their own preparation for the instructional day. Faculty or department meetings were being held before school instead of after school, and teachers found that they were fresher for thinking through difficult curriculum issues and had greater energy to be engaged in professional discussions. Two suburban teachers noted that they had time to incorporate the most recent world events into their daily social studies and economics lessons because they had time to go to the Internet each morning before classes began. Will the overall effect of a later start be to improve instruction and student achievement? That question is being studied at this time, and we may have some answers within the next year.

Impact on teachers' personal lives. The professional and personal lives of teachers are unquestionably interdependent, and the findings from the focus groups highlighted the need to ask more definitively about teachers' personal lives on the written questionnaire. Fifty-one percent of the respondents agreed or strongly agreed with the statement "I have found that the later start time has had a positive impact on my personal schedule *before* school." Thirty-four percent disagreed or strongly disagreed, and only 14% were neutral. By contrast, 68% disagreed or strongly disagreed with the statement "I have found that the later start time has had a positive impact on my personal schedule *after* school" (with 49% of that total at the strongly disagree level). Sixteen percent were neutral, and 16% agreed or strongly agreed.

Those teachers who experienced a positive personal outcome from the later start cited improved health, more personal family time in the morning, greater alertness in the morning, and time to exercise in the morning before going to work. The fact that they were getting more sleep and were better rested was brought up by 16% of the teachers. One stated, "I did not get more and more exhausted as the year progressed as I formerly did," while another reflected, "I realized in May that in years past I've been totally sleep deprived and acted as such!"

The negative outcomes from the later start were a strong theme in the focus groups and were even slightly more prevalent on the written questionnaire. The most often mentioned personal reason for disliking the later starting time was that it resulted in having to drive in heavier traffic both to and from school. Teachers also reported being more tired at the end of the day than in previous years. The combination of personal obligations and teacher fatigue was perceived by Minneapolis faculty members as having decreased teacher supervision of after-school activities.

Overall view of the high school changes. The teachers were asked to complete the statement "My feelings, overall, about the later start are . . ." with one of the following responses: "Hate it," "Don't like it," "Neutral," "Like it," or "Love it." Only slightly more respondents (45%) chose "like it" or "love it" than chose "don't like it" or "hate it" (44%). Only 11% felt neutral. As for the strongest responses, 23% chose "love it," and 15% chose "hate it."

Finally, the following question was asked: What would be the ideal starting time for school? Although 44% of respondents had said that they either hated or did not like the new starting time, the responses to this question made it clear that very few (3.5%) wanted to return to the previous starting time of 7:15 a.m. The most popular time for Minneapolis high schools to start, according to these teachers, was 8 a.m. (See Figure 1.) Indeed, almost three-quarters of the teachers surveyed (72.7%) chose a starting time of 8 a.m. or later.

Findings from the Middle Schools

Probably the most difficult transition made in the Minneapolis school system was the shift to a 9:40 a.m. start for the middle schools. Overall, the general opinion among school personnel in the focus groups was that the 9:40 start did not provide a sufficient amount of "prime time" learning in the morning. Although a few commented that they were better able to handle discipline problems and that students were more alert and doing better, the majority of teachers reported students to be more difficult to motivate at the end of the day as a result of student and teacher fatigue. Fatigue was also perceived to contribute to impatience and decreased effectiveness in managing student behavior. In general, teachers felt that they were working harder and accomplishing less.

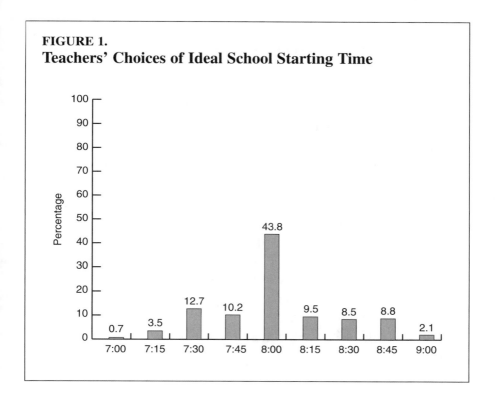

FIGURE 1.
Teachers' Choices of Ideal School Starting Time

The later ending of the school day limited the time available for teachers to attend to personal business and appointments. This made it necessary for some to leave school early or to request a substitute for the day. Because it was difficult to find substitutes who would teach late in the day and because some businesses were closed after school, teachers occasionally had to use their prep time and, in some cases, their sick days.

Teachers also noted that students involved in after-school activities often needed to leave class early, missing all or part of their last academic period and disrupting learning for others. Activities were simply too late in the day, and the time remaining after school was too short. There was a perception that, because of safety concerns, fewer middle school students were participating in after-school activities. One teacher reported that two students dropped out of the student council because their parents said that it was too dangerous for them to walk in the neighborhood at 7 p.m. Because the workday for staff members concluded almost immediately after students were dismissed, parents were unable to contact the school for help if there was a problem with a late or missed bus. One support staff person suggested that the unavailability of school personnel after school hours had fostered adversarial relationships between parents and the school. Safety was also a concern in the morning, when parents left for work and students had to get themselves off to school.

Teachers who were willing and able to stay later during the first year of the change noted that fewer students stayed after school for tutoring and that before-school options were viable only for certain students. "I used to have students staying after school every week getting help," said one teacher. "Now I have no one staying after to get help. The only kids who can get help are those who can get a ride in the mornings. So it ends up being the privileged getting the help, and those who are not privileged have more and more barriers."

Like the high schools, the middle schools — third on the three-tiered busing system — had to deal with late buses. Transportation problems were seen to affect student attendance, classroom learning, field trips, the length of after-school activities, and even district initiatives such as optional morning reading programs.

A bright spot to report in this picture is the finding of one of the middle school students who, for his "research" class, designed a survey to assess the students' opinions of the later start. To his surprise, a majority of his peers favored the later start. They noted that they were less tired for class in the morning and that learning was easier. Certainly, there is a need to have a more representative sample before generalizing from this student's "findings." Nevertheless, both the teachers and the MPS school board are interested in further assessing the opinions of the student body before considering any change back to the earlier starting time.

Findings from the Elementary Schools

The 14 elementary schools participating in the study experienced various starting times. Two of the schools moved from a 9:40 start to a 7:40 start, a two-hour change. All other schools experienced a one-hour shift in starting time. Two schools included in the elementary sample were elementary/middle schools serving kindergarten through eighth grade. At the elementary level, we conducted focus groups only with teachers and administrators and not with students.

Elementary teachers from the five schools that moved from an 8:40 to a 9:40 start cited a variety of areas negatively affected by the later start. Similar to the middle school responses, these areas included teaching, busing/transportation, end of the school day, student behavior, meetings, after-school activities, safety, and personal schedules.

The areas that generated the most feedback were the negative effect the later start had on teaching and learning in the shortened morning and student fatigue and disengagement in the afternoon. With the 9:40 start, academic programs often did not begin until 10 a.m., after buses arrived and students ate breakfast at school. Teachers unanimously agreed that third-tier buses were chronically late. Also, students often came to school having already watched up to three hours of television in the morning, since most young children who go to bed early tend to wake early as well. One teacher described such children as having "eyes glazed over." Clearly, to the faculty and staff in these focus groups, the very late start had no apparent benefits for the elementary-aged child.

In contrast to those schools that moved from an 8:40 to a 9:40 start, teachers at elementary schools that experienced the reverse, moving from a 9:40 to an 8:40 start, reported a positive impact on the beginning and end of the school day. Students' energy and learning levels were higher in the morning and lasted throughout the day. The earlier school start meant fewer before-school transitions for students (e.g., from day care to school), and it seemed to capture students when they were at their best for learning. One teacher reported, "Last year I had a student who was in day care at 6:30 a.m. By the time she came to school at 9:30 a.m., her day was over. That's just too long for kids to be up in the morning. I feel this year the kids are much better, ready to learn when they come to school. And throughout the whole school day, I still feel that they are alert and ready to learn, and I didn't feel that way last year."

The 8:40 start had a positive impact on after-school activities as well. With an earlier school ending, parents were more inclined to allow their children to participate in extracurricular activities because they did not have to miss classes to attend events, and they arrived home earlier, lessening concerns about safety. Students were reported to have more time for homework, play, and after-school academic help.

The 8:40 start was also positive for teachers personally and professionally. Most of the teachers said that they felt more relaxed, less rushed, and more energized to teach. They had time to supervise after-school activities, attend workshops, and keep personal appointments without taking time off from school.

Responses from support and administrative staff at the elementary schools that started at 8:40 confirmed teacher perspectives that students were more alert and ready to learn. The earlier start increased morning instructional time, which was viewed as advantageous to elementary-aged students, especially children with emotional and behavioral disorders. Staff members reported that fewer students left school early for appointments, and this resulted in less lost instructional time and fewer class disruptions. Students had more opportunities to participate in after-school activities, and more took advantage of them. School climate was perceived to have improved from the previous year; morale among staff members was considered to be high, and the pace of the school was less hectic and more peaceful. Being second, as opposed to third, on the tiered busing schedule was an improvement and allowed adequate time for staff members to manage special events and address parental concerns about their children.

Elementary teachers from the two schools that experienced a two-hour change in starting time, moving from 9:40 to 7:40, reported that the earlier start had a negative impact on student attendance/tardies, the beginning of the school day, school climate, and after-school activities. Even with school-purchased alarm clocks provided to some families, students were still absent often, making it difficult to teach with only three-fourths of the class present. Transportation constraints and the early start also shortened student field trips.

Unlike the teachers, support staff and administrative staff members reported that the 7:40 start had a positive impact on teaching, on the end of the school day, and on after-school activities. These staff members perceived students to be "more on task and focused" during the day, which contributed to fewer afternoon behavior problems. Students with ADHD (attention deficit hyperactivity disorder) were seen to have benefited from the earlier schedule, although some reservations were expressed about what kind of an impact increased absences and tardies were having on learning. More students were also taking advantage of after-school activities, but bus schedules determined the length of after-school practices and events.

Teachers from the three elementary schools that moved from 8:40 to 7:40 commented on a number of positive effects. Children appeared to be more alert at the beginning of the day and stayed more energized throughout the day. Students experienced fewer morning transitions and were more ready to learn. Teachers perceived themselves and their students to be more patient and productive in the afternoon. Fewer behavior problems contributed to a calm, positive school environment, and student participation in after-school activities seemed to have increased. Being first on the tiered busing schedule meant that buses arrived promptly at the beginning and end of the school day. The early start was also considered beneficial for afternoon kindergarten classes because children actually arrived at school late in the morning as opposed to the afternoon. Support and administrative staff members at the schools starting at 7:40 a.m. concurred with the teachers and had relatively few complaints about moving to the earlier time.

Discussion

When compared with the suburban case study, the structural factors operating in the MPS seem to be magnified by the issue of starting time. The socioeconomic advantages for the suburban students meant that they could get transportation to receive before-school academic help and that they had opportunities for greater participation in school-related activities. Any inconveniences associated with the change in starting time were viewed as "workable" situations, and options, alternatives, and flexibility in scheduling were seen as available. Moreover, the later ending to the school day and subsequent participation in after-school activities did not raise concerns about student safety in the suburban context.

Clearly, the least desirable and most problematic start time was the 9:40 start at the middle schools and at some elementary schools. Teaching and learning were considered to be significantly compromised. Instruction did not begin until late in the morning, pushing academics into the afternoon, when students were reported to be less alert and less interested in learning. Teachers also had to contend with students leaving to attend events and appointments. The later ending to the school day meant that fewer students and faculty members were involved in after-school activities and that parents were more concerned about students arriving home late, when it was particularly unsafe.

There was an underlying assumption that earlier school starting times (e.g., 7:40 and 8:40) were inherently better because they were more consistent with "real life" and the typical adult work pattern. The 9:40 start seemed to communicate to personnel and students that learning was not a priority. The 8:40 start was seen to capture elementary students' prime learning time. Although there were mixed responses from elementary schools about the 7:40 start, it resulted in fewer morning transitions for students, who arrived better prepared to learn.

The impact on the community of the changes in starting times remains unclear and will require further research. What is evident from the findings to date is that students are listening to the debate about school starting time and are affected by it.

Because only one full year has elapsed since the MPS changed its starting times, data will need to be collected over the next several years to more fully understand the effects of a later start on school life and student learning. Differences in culture, socioeconomic status, gender, and other areas need to be studied to determine how various subpopulations are affected. Observational, performance, and self-reported data will continue to be very helpful in understanding the link between schedules and learning outcomes. Several key pieces of data already collected by schools (e.g., grades, test scores, attendance, and behavioral reports) might help define an optimal starting time for school.

Conclusion

The findings of the CAREI study raise questions about whether a universal starting time or a flexible one is best for students. It is unlikely that any one schedule could accommodate the needs of all stakeholders. Given this fact, the district could investigate the possibility of creating flexible schedules so as to offer viable options for students, families, and school personnel. Several respondents to the high school teachers' questionnaire spontaneously made such suggestions.

- "I would rather restructure the school day and schedule. Provide more learning (not just credit makeup or remediation) for students after 2 p.m. — especially courses that are interdisciplinary."
- "Flexible starts/endings would be ideal."
- "At the high school, flexible starting time should be an option. Athletes need the early time. Students who work need the early start, morning people like the early start, but others benefit from the later start."
- "I think we should have an early start and a late start. Have school start at 7:15 for those who want to come then and another start at 9:15 for those who like it late. Everyone goes a full six periods, but the early ones get out two hours sooner (or take an extra class). There certainly are enough students and staff who would like both start times."

One teacher noted, "The 7:15 a.m. starting time was a death knell for period 1 (and often period 2)." The research on adolescent sleep patterns is indicating that some change in school starting times may be beneficial. In districts that rely on multi-tiered busing, planning for the middle and elementary grades must be part of any overall strategy.

Educators who have experienced the change to a later start as positive speak forcefully about its impact. "Even though the change in starting time has affected after-school activities, I feel that the benefits — of having school hours more tuned in to 'teenage clocks' — are significant," said one teacher. Another commented, "If you are involved in any kind of after-school activity, it can be difficult to take care of personal business, but the positives for the kids outweigh this single personal consideration." And finally, a word of caution from a teacher about hasty decisions in any direction: "This change has been a long time in coming — please give it a long trial before making a judgment."

The effects on teaching and learning are only beginning to emerge. If we are to know anything of substance, the medical and educational research into this issue and its outcomes must continue for several years to come.

Notes

1. Kyla Wahlstrom and Carol Freeman, "Executive Summary of Findings from School Start Time Study," 1997, available from http://carei.coled.umn.edu.

KYLA L. WAHLSTROM
30-MINUTE VIDEOTAPE

Kyla L. Wahlstrom discusses her work on adolescent sleep needs and school starting time issues with Phillip Harris, director of the Center for Professional Development and Services at Phi Delta Kappa International.

"Our objective was to go beyond the article," comments Harris. Data that became available after publication of the article is included in the discussion. "The effects of sleep deprivation in adolescence are pervasive, and the discussion should give teachers insights that will inform education policy and practice."

30-minute videotape
$29.95 (PDK members, $19.95) + s&h

ORDER BY PHONE: 1-800-766-1156
Major credit cards accepted.

Or send an institutional purchase order to Phi Delta Kappa International, P.O. Box 789, Bloomington, IN 47402-0789. Include $5 shipping and handling charge for each video. Indiana residents add 5% sales tax. Purchase orders and credit card orders also are accepted by fax at (812) 339-0018.